CHRIST *over* culture

Raising Christian Kids to
Stand in a Postmodern World

ANDREA CRUM

First printing: May 2024

New Leaf Press, P.O. Box 726, Green Forest, AR 72638

New Leaf Press is a division of the New Leaf Publishing Group, LLC.

ISBN: 978-0-89221-770-0

ISBN: 978-1-61458-898-6 (digital)

Library of Congress Control Number: 2024935739

Cover: Diana Bogardus Interior: Terry White

Printed in the United States of America

Please visit our website for other great titles:

www.masterbooks.com

For information regarding promotional opportunities, please contact the publicity department at pr@nlpg.com.

Contents

Endorsements

"In a straightforward, easy to understand way, Andrea teaches us about the influences that have shaped our culture into what it is today. But she doesn't leave us hopeless and defeated. In *Christ Over Culture*, Andrea gives us a clear roadmap to equipping our kids to live confidently and make an impact for Christ. This book is a must-read guide for parents."

—Kathy Gibbens
Host of the *Filter It Through a Brain Cell* podcast

"By providing the framework for the postmodern worldview and critical theory ideas and countering it with the Biblical perspective, Andrea offers clarity, direction, and inspiration as we seek to equip the next generation toward faithfulness and courage."

—Alisha Illian
Author of *Chasing Perfect*

"This book is like a Christian parenting lifehack. Navigating the mish-mash of cultural ideas as a Kingdom-minded parent is no easy job. Luckily, Andrea has created a resource which will greatly unburden your efforts. Her insightful analysis of culture is clear and compelling, while her prescriptions for Christian parents are easy to follow and theologically sound. It's evident in her writing that she brings a sincere heart to this project, as well as a practical approach to helping parents conceptualize the principles of the Christian worldview, and its competitors, so they can effectively disciple their families."

—Lori Morrow
VP of Women in Apologetics

Introduction

What will your kids say when asked, "How many genders are there?" like my son was asked in seventh grade by a couple of kids in the hall on his way to class.

Will they know the answer? Will they be able to articulate a response? Should they be able to?

Over the years, I've struggled with the idea that our inclination is to raise martyrs rather than kids. It's as if this unwritten expectation exists that our kids must make up for the battles we lost, the conversations we weren't brave enough to have, and the apathy we let settle on our faith.

We can turn on any given TV show, scroll through any news feed, listen in on any teen conversation, and see that the world our kids are growing up in is vastly different from the one we did. We also recognize that the battles our kids will encounter will be monumentally more challenging than the ones we faced. The world isn't pretty out there, and the hostility toward Christians who hold biblical beliefs tends to be trending up rather than leveling out. Some theologians call this not just a postmodern society our kids are growing up in, but a post-Christian one.

So, in this "Strange New World,"[1] as author Carl Trueman calls it, should our kids be martyrs? Not literal martyrs like the first-century Christians, but metaphorical martyrs who put themselves out there in the hallway of seventh grade and proclaim to the world — or at least proclaim to the unforgiving, unrelenting teen universe — that there are only two genders, only one way to procreate and produce life, that an XX chromosome for females and XY chromosome for males is in every cell of our bodies, and no amount of hormone pills or surgeries can change that.

In other words, do our kids have to make up for our silence?

When we think about the world our kids are growing up in, it's natural to lament, to mourn because it shouldn't be this way, to recognize that, yes, we, and the generations before us, had a part to play in all this. But we can't stay in a place where sadness turns to fear and our most instinctual response to stick our heads in the sand prevails. Instead, we pull ourselves up, look to the One ultimately in control, and find solace in the knowledge that this cultural moment we find ourselves in doesn't surprise God. He's not worried about whether the Christian faith will make it. Jesus Himself even declared that the gates of hell would not prevail against His Church (Matthew 16:18).

So, we remind ourselves that today is a new day, and where we lacked intention in the past, we can make up for it in the here and now. God can use His supernatural power to move in us and our children in ways to make up for lost time and exponentially increase it.

Resisting the temptation to raise martyrs rather than set-apart Christian kids, we remind ourselves that Jesus already won. He overcame the world. He knows how the story unfolds and how our children's lives will be part of it.

Our kids are HIS handiwork, created in Christ Jesus to do good works, which God prepared for them to do (Ephesians 2:10). He marked out each one of their times in history and the territories for them to live (Acts 17:26). He is not an abstract or absent Father, but One who knows our children better and loves them more than we ever will.

God gave us our children to guide, lead, steward, protect, disciple, mentor, and give them a firm foundation of the faith so that they will stand even when the pressure of the world begs them to worship superficial idols and compromise their faith. Even in the chaos, they will remain faithful to God and fortified to stand like Shadrach, Meshach, and Abednego in the fiery furnace, not to be "*tossed back and forth ... and blown here and there by every wind of teaching and ... the craftiness of people in their deceitful scheming*" (Ephesians 4:14).

God is doing something beautiful in this next generation. He is raising up a generation of believers who will not bow down to other "gods," a generation who will stand firm on His truth and on His Word, who will walk in His way, who will follow in obedience and declare His truth from the rooftops, who will not be silent, who will raise their voices and declare His majesty.

And you and I are raising them.

God knew His plans for this coming generation. He knew we would be the parents to shepherd them. He knew we'd heed the call, we'd make the sacrifice, we'd find the strength and make the time. He knew we would raise them to stand.

1

The Missing *Plot*

When I started in ministry, I began having regular chats with women. It was a wonderful way to build relationships, learn what God was doing in these women's lives, and learn more about their beliefs. Over chai lattes and conversations spanning everything from purpose to politics to children, I found that about half of these Christian women believed homosexuality was okay.

"Love is love, right?" was a typical response. The realization confused me, mostly because I assumed that as Christians, we would all be on the same page about God's design and, more importantly, the core Christian tenets of sin and salvation. Yet, I stumbled into discussions with women, specifically moms, who had no issue with what was either a glaring contradiction in their faith or, more likely, an unrealized compromise.

Either way, something was off, and research confirmed what I was experiencing. Many Christians today do not align with the beliefs that the Christian faith has held for thousands of years. Worse yet, pastors, including youth pastors, follow suit, with only 37% of pastors and 12% of youth pastors holding to a biblical worldview, according to research out of Arizona Christian University.

At one point, my oldest son felt God's call to start a Bible study. He came home one day excited because his friend seemed just as on fire for God as he was. He even hoped this kid could lead the Bible study with him. We talked about the importance of making sure this young man believed the same thing about sin and salvation as our son did. The topic of LGBTQ+ is always a good litmus test.

Imagine our son's disappointment when he learned that although his friend believed homosexuality was ultimately not God's design, his friend also had strong beliefs that we must respect each person's choices, "just love everybody," and let them live the way they want without interference or correction, even if they self-identify as Christians.

Then there is a ministry I had long believed was a Jesus-loving, Scripture-believing, truth-telling organization. Over time, however, I heard rumblings of a support group implemented for LGBTQ+-identifying teens. I initially reasoned that this ministry was well-intentioned in its desire to help these teens escape the lifestyle. However, this support group soon evolved into a group of teens affirming each other in the LGBTQ+ lifestyle.

A couple of years later, this same ministry taught on reimagining what it meant to be a Christian, focusing solely on Jesus' love as His only characteristic.

As compelling as the teaching was, and as much as I wanted to fall into complete alignment with this leader's point that the Christian

Church was not always acting like Christ and that love should be a cornerstone of our interactions with people, what kept nagging at me was that this intriguing narrative missed the plot.

I encountered the same situation with a faith-based organization promising to teach churches how to engage teens who identify as LGBTQ+. Hearing how they developed relationships with these students and shared God's love made me tear up. In many ways, it mirrored what God had been clear with us about in our ministry. We were not only to declare the biblical standard for what was right and wrong in society but also to be the hands and feet of Jesus in a culture influenced by the sexual revolution. That meant loving people who often felt unloved by the Church.

What I noticed, however, was that, once again, they buried the lead and, worse yet, missed the plot.

In all these situations, while professing to believe the Bible on the topic of God's design for the genders and for sex in marriage, not anywhere did they mention the moment of truth – the moment when they finally shared with these individuals about sin and the true gospel of Christ. The gospel of Jesus tells us we are all sinners who have fallen short of the glory of God and that God required, ever since the Garden with Adam and Eve, a perfect blood sacrifice to atone for our sins (Genesis 3:21). Jesus' death on the Cross, the shedding of His blood, was God's ultimate justice on display, freeing a dying world from death and setting us into freedom from sin and healing from hurt for all those who believe and follow our One true risen Lord, not only in salvation but also in obedience to His commands.

Silence, in the name of sharing God's love, only leaves people in their brokenness and sin, instead of in the freedom, healing, hope, and joy that comes from a life of following Christ.

God's love directly ties to sin and salvation, "But God demonstrates his own love for us in this: While we were still sinners, Christ died for us" (Romans 5:8). If we miss this, we miss the Gospel.

This insistence on God's love as His only attribute has, in many ways, made the gospel of Jesus null and void in the Christian Church. If God's character excludes His order, holiness, justice, judgment, wrath, and grace, then Jesus' sacrifice on the Cross was not necessary.

So, how did we get to this place where the one true gospel of Jesus Christ has been hijacked and reimagined?

It would be easy to pinpoint the barrage of cultural influences and assume that those caused it. For example:

- Our desensitization to all the LGBTQ+ messages that have bombarded us over the last twenty years in every sector of entertainment we consume, from books to TV shows, movies, and social media.
- The legalization of same-sex marriage in the Obergefell v. Hodges case and the number of people we know who celebrated their legal right to love whoever they chose.
- All the new Diversity, Equity, and Inclusion (DEI) efforts finding their way into businesses, and sadly, some churches that taught about the oppression of some and the importance of making sure everyone felt safe and included.

Many Christian thinkers would also tell us the cause is our culture's obsession with self. In other words, we are the center of our universe, and God is part of our world instead of us being part of His. In his book *Strange New World*, Carl Trueman chronicles the past couple hundred years of intellectual and philosophical thinkers who have paved the way to our current understanding of self, which includes how our culture now understands, and even accepts, the modern-day belief that we can disassociate our minds from our bodies, as seen with the transgender movement.[2]

One of the most eye-opening realizations came from Alisa Childers' book *Another Gospel*. It highlighted the reimagining of the Christian faith by the progressive movement infiltrating Christian thought. Her insights and experience illuminated why our churches are struggling and, ultimately, shrinking, according to Gallup research, and how the postmodern worldview is setting up shop in the Christian Church.[3] With prominent themes of church hurt, deconstructionists turned exvangelicals, and churches flying rainbow flags, something has definitely changed.

But what exactly?

If we examine the last several decades, we can uncover three reasons why the Church was vulnerable to the diminishing and dulling of the Christian faith that we see today and, more importantly, our understanding and articulation of the one true gospel.

These areas are essential for course correction as we raise our kids to stand.

2

The Dulling Begins

As a mom now in my forties, I still remember the church I attended in fourth grade. We had never attended church before, but my mom decided my brother and I needed a positive Christian influence, so off we went one Sunday morning.

It wasn't until the church's summer camp in seventh grade that I believed Christ as my Savior and felt the Holy Spirit in my life. I was on cloud nine for a few days and experienced an overwhelming peace. Not long after, though, the teenage life consumed me. I slowly slipped away, having never been discipled in the faith, into everyday teen drama, which eventually led to sinful behavior and a questioning of my faith by the time I entered my late teens.

Over time, I found my way back to Christ through one particular friend and the prayers of countless people. God is faithful to bring us back when we go astray or when our faith isn't mature and our walk isn't thriving. The sad thing is that I got lost again years later. Not the lost that isn't saved, but the lost that goes off track, meanders off the narrow road, and finds other things more appealing in life than Jesus. That indifference toward my walk with the Lord lasted around twenty years.

So, why did this happen? Moreover, why is my story similar to so many other people I know? Maybe even yours. If we take a trip down memory lane, we can uncover three primary vulnerabilities in the Church and Christian living that led us to this place.

1. Lack of Discipleship

One of the seemingly greatest inventions in the Church was the mass production of cute resources that helped us to quickly and efficiently share the gospel. Armed with our bracelets, cubes, and pamphlets, we set out to evangelize the world one neighborhood at a time.

For the most part, the gospel presentation shared about our separation from God by sin and how Jesus paid the price for our sins on the Cross, and if we did as Romans 10:9 says, *"If you confess with your mouth, 'Jesus is Lord,' and believe in your heart that God raised him from the dead, you will be saved."* Many who liked what they heard prayed, accepted Christ into their hearts, and went on with their lives.

While full of good intentions to help a busy Christian society share the gospel easily, following Jesus requires more than a prayer and minimizing the gospel to a few verses shared in a three-minute presentation. This introduction to the faith doesn't express the breadth of what Jesus calls us to when we trust Him as Lord and Savior. Now, we have a whole generation of Christians who grew up on this commoditized gospel.

Jesus tells us in no uncertain terms that to follow Him is to believe, repent, take up our cross, count the costs, walk the narrow road, live a life of obedience and sacrifice, and understand that the world will hate us because it first hated Him.

When we read Romans 10:9 in context, we discover that the preceding verses tell us that we receive righteousness by faith by having the Word of God in our hearts and minds. Verses 6–8 reference Deuteronomy 30, with God saying that to follow, honor, and love Him is to obey Him. So, when we read Romans 10:9 in context, there is already an expectation that we will obey and follow God along with our belief and declaration of faith in Him.

Somehow, we miss this part of the gospel story. We talk about how Jesus is our Savior but neglect that Jesus is our Lord.

In the Great Commission, Jesus ultimately called us to make disciples. The word disciple in Hebrew means "learners" or "scholars." When we make disciples, we teach people to know God, know His ways, and obey. Jesus even tells us to teach *"them to obey everything I have commanded you"* (Matthew 28:20).

Our lack of discipleship has hurt the Church because we do not know what we believe, and we do not know how to defend it. It has created a weakened immunity in our defenses and allowed for ideas that do not glorify God to enter the Church and, in some cases, our homes.

The good news is that we can create changes in our own families. There is no better place to make disciples than at home with our kids. They are our priority, the ones God has given us to steward, so we should start there.

I say that, but for many years, the idea that we as parents need to disciple our kids made my throat tight and my shoulders tense. Anyone else?

With our busy schedules, lack of discipleship and knowledge of God's Word, the prospect of discipling our kids can get overwhelming quickly. And what do we do when we get overwhelmed? Change the scenery. We scroll, grab that glass of wine, text a friend, or do anything to distract us from the reminder that we should be doing something we aren't.

This leads to the second vulnerability in the Church for most believers.

2. Distractions Galore!

After spending some time away from the Lord in my late teens, I found my way back through a friend who invited me to play in a softball league at her church. Meeting all the softball players and getting invited back to church by a few of them eventually led me to the pew on Sunday mornings. Rededicating my life was an easy decision to make, and for the most part, it filled me with peace, with only the occasional longing for my old sinful life.

Within the next couple of years, as I got my faith walk back on track, I met my future husband. Our friendship grew on a church trip to Europe, and over that next year, we fell in love. Soon, we married, bought a house, and had many fun vacations. Seven years later, our first child arrived. Three years after that, our second made his debut.

In the meantime, my career was blowing up in the best way possible — money and promotions and travel overseas. My husband became a stay-at-home dad, and I became the sole provider.

Within a decade, we moved from our starter home to our forever home. Life was good. Life was busy. It was the dream, right? Big home, lots of money, positional prestige at work. Yeah, life was going well.

Only it wasn't. Stressed all the time, pressure to provide, desire to do all the things everyone else was doing, demands at work for more, no light at the end of the tunnel, a waning spiritual life, a son who called out more for his dad than for me, and a budding alcohol addiction to numb the stress.

The truth is hard to admit. It's even harder to type out loud for the world to see. But there it is — life and all its distractions, and our constant desire for more, buried me, tearing me farther and farther away from Christ. Soon, I was that Sunday Christian I used to feel sorry for.

It's here where I found myself in the second stint of my wilderness season. Only it lasted a lot longer than the first.

My story is likely similar to yours. Maybe the activities are different — school sports, over-volunteering, the fifteenth load of laundry, anyone? Maybe it's not the wife but the husband who is consumed with work and always gone. Maybe the numbing is something else, like food, pills, porn, the gym, shopping, or scrolling. For the most part, the average Christian attending our churches today lives burnt out, overwhelmed, and exhausted, even if it doesn't look that way on the outside, because we live in a world that preaches conventional wisdom and not godly wisdom.

Go, go, go, earn more and more, buy bigger, save for that future you're not guaranteed. All this instead of coming to Jesus, who promises to give us rest, trusting that God will take care of all our earthly needs and storing for ourselves treasures in heaven rather than on earth, where moths and vermin cannot consume and thieves cannot break in and steal.

We get distracted from the things that matter most. The Kingdom. Our relationship with Christ. The purpose God calls us to, including discipling our children.

What if the most significant work of the enemy over the last several decades in the Church was to lead us to contempt for ordinary lives and peaceful living and instead lead us toward busy, unsustainable chaos that always promised more but never really delivered?

When we don't have time to pour into others, including our kids, something central to God's desire for our lives and family and crucial to Christian living is lost.

If we don't have time to disciple our kids, then there aren't many pillars of faith rising right now to hold up the Church in all biblical truth and love in this next generation, which means our foundation is weak and our grip on the Church, as a whole, is slipping.

But how can we disciple if we don't know what we're doing?

We are now to our third vulnerability.

3. Unchanged

The wise youth pastor at our church told me once that this next generation focuses more on whether Christianity is good than whether it is true. He said they would determine if it was true once they decided it was good. They determine a good Christian life by a godly life well-lived, not a life well-imagined. Kids can sniff out hypocrisy a million miles away. If they see us espouse a belief on Sunday mornings and social media that we don't adhere to in our own lives, then it leaves them with no real idea of what genuine faith is and what it promises to believers — a changed life.

I'm not talking about a successful, rich, or easy-going life; I'm talking about a life where love, joy, peace, patience, kindness, gentleness, goodness, faithfulness, and self-control are thriving and commonplace (Galatians 5:22-23). I'm also not talking about a perfect, self-righteous life, but one where grace abounds, forgiveness heals, and daily surrender is a regular practice.

Jesus promises us a changed and forgiven life. One that leaves the conventions of this world and follows Him. One where the old sinful life is no more, and we are a new creation. A life where spiritual gifts exist, fruits of the Spirit are ripening and flourishing, and there is a perspective that sees how well God clothes the lilies of the field and how the peace that surpasses all understanding is present when we set our eyes squarely on Him.

How many of us live this life? I sure didn't for most of my Christian walk, and even now, there are some days when I'm in the middle of the chaos, distracted and spiritually empty, nudging myself to remember what God has for me in the quiet of His presence.

You see, we disciple from the full well; we pour out from what we have and the life we have lived, from our experience seeing the goodness of the Lord, walking with Him in the trial, climbing with Him out of the pit, and studying the Scriptures with intention. Sadly, many of our wells have been in drought for decades, and we have nothing to give and even less to teach, so we don't disciple.

There was a moment when I recognized the incongruency in my life and, ultimately, my hypocrisy. I realized that there was one Andrea people knew at work, and another Andrea people knew at church. The one at work had high expectations and drive and lacked empathy. The one at church was full of smiles, mercy, and love. I was a church greeter after all.

I even remember a team dinner while traveling to Europe for a work trip when I mentioned I was a Christian, and one of my colleagues said, "Oh, I didn't know you were one of those." Hadn't he seen my worship playlist?

That comment stayed with me for a long time. My colleague's statement about "being one of those" dripped with contempt for Christians, and I justified it was a compliment. That somehow, as a firm believer, I infiltrated common culture without detection. Thankfully, I wasn't holier than thou and could fit in with the world. In the world, but not of the world, right?

It took me a long time to admit that he didn't see me any differently than a non-believer. Maybe it was my hard-working, no-nonsense, "projects are more important than people" attitude. Or maybe it was because I liked my third glass of wine too much.

Either way, my life did not reflect Christ.

Can you relate?

The Christian faith promises change because Jesus saves and the Holy Spirit transforms. If we look more like the world, love what the world loves, and believe what the world says is true, then the transformation (aka sanctification) process stalls or altogether stops until we put the One true God back on the throne where He belongs and align our lives back to Him and His Word.

We live more fulfilling lives when we dig into our relationship with Christ, surrender to Him in all ways, and allow Him to transform us into His image. When we do, we also give our children a glimpse into the life God has for us. One that is good, not easy or trauma-free, but full of peace because we know our help comes from the Creator of heaven and earth.

If we remain unchanged, the world has nothing to look for in the darkness. Likewise, if all that people experience are Christians jaded by the political environment and progressive agendas who don't reflect the love of Christ in our interactions, then we aren't presenting the changed life that the gospel promises.

Our kids are desperate to see a Christian life that fulfills its promises, and our dark and dying world is desperate to see that city on a hill that cannot be hidden; to see our light, goodness, joy, and peace; and to encounter Christians who let their changed life shine rather than get dull and dim.

God calls us to get discipled, focus on Him, and change. The implications of this trifecta of lack of discipleship, distractions, and unchanged lives are evident in the Church today. These are some of the most important reasons why the Church is in a weakened state today, why progressive ideology has taken root in some churches, and why only 4 percent of Gen Z has a biblical worldview.[4] We need intentionality in these areas for our children's faith's sake if we ever expect to see change.

3

New Day Rising

Some people say that our culture is lost and that there is no getting it back or reversing this freight train that will completely break down every moral and physical standard we have for what it means to be humans made in the image of God. The implication is that we will be like Europe, with empty churches that people visit as relics instead of places of worship.

It's tempting to agree, especially when scrolling through my news feed.

Then I remember something so significant and seemingly radical that we can never forget ... Jesus only had twelve disciples. He only had twelve, and they changed the world. They didn't just make a dent; they left a mark of seismic proportions that changed all of mankind for the last two thousand years.

Ultimately, I refuse to believe our culture is lost. If I did, I'd crawl into a fetal position and never get up. That's not what God called us to do. He called us to GO, to make disciples, to have dominion over this earth and rule over it, to be salt and light, and to live in this world and not be of it.

There's such freedom, confidence, purpose, meaning, authority, and joy in a life like this, and since this is the life that God has called us to, we can trust Him to go before us as we walk through this culture and raise our kids in it.

Someone said once, "Satan should have learned by now that if he wants a weak Church, he shouldn't persecute it." These powerful words speak to the determination that wells up in us when we, as Christian parents, feel attacked, and more specifically, when our children are under attack.

Isn't that why you're reading this book? It's why I'm writing it. I understand the hour in which we are living. I sense the urgency. I see what's coming up ahead, and I'm not willing to sit it out, and I bet you aren't either.

Our jobs as parents have never been more necessary. We have to preserve the faith, prepare our kids, and pray. To act with intention and disciple our children.

Yet, here we are, parents attempting to raise Christian kids in a chaotic culture, and for many of us, our relationship with God is weak, and our biblical understanding is shallow. We are watching the future of the Christian faith slip away right before our eyes. We worry for our kids, are weary of the world, and are overwhelmed because we know it's our problem to solve, but we don't know how to solve it.

The temptation is to do what we all do when fear strikes.

Some of us freeze. We stick our heads in the sand and pretend that if we don't pay attention, or don't talk to our kids about what's happening in the world, or that if we can keep our kids busy enough, then this postmodern culture will pass them by without even a scratch.

Some of us flee. We've bought our land in the country, we're growing our crops, we may have even thrown out the TV, and we've taken every measure to protect our kids from the world that seeks to kill, steal, and destroy. We believe that if we remove our kids from the world, then they will be safe from the destruction ahead.

Some of us fight. We've gotten angry with the world, our frustration seeps out in every conversation, and we roll our eyes and tell our kids about the woke indoctrination that is destroying our country. We won't leave culture. We will fight with all we have to salvage what we can — with pitchforks, if necessary.

I've been there. I've had these fears, thought these thoughts, and met many parents who have, too. The good news is that we don't have to live this way. We can parent in freedom, truth, and love, and teach our kids to live a life that does the same.

We can remind ourselves daily who is ultimately in control, surrender to His authority, and parent in a way that is intentional in focus and Holy Spirit–led.

Parenting our kids in this confusing culture with Christ-fueled freedom is what we are talking about in this book because one thing is for certain: equipped parents equip their kids. Knowledge is power, as they say, and an understanding of the world your kids are growing up in, educating them on it, and walking through it with them, along with a strong foundation of Scripture, is the most powerful way to raise kids who will stand firm in their faith.

It's no mistake that you're parenting your kids during this cultural crisis we are experiencing. God knew His plans for your family when He placed you and your kids here during this time in history. For many of us, the way forward from here will now require a change of pace, priorities, and perspective.

Pace – The speed at which we are moving in our lives

How many people in your life can you name who aren't busy? From school carpool lines and parent-teacher conferences, or homeschool activities to sporting games and practices, to church on Sunday and Wednesday, to volunteering, to family fun nights, time with friends, and date night with your boo, not to mention all the activities associated with work too — late night conference calls, anyone?

We are all moving at an extra fast pace. We jam-pack our days with stuff. Some of it is valuable. Actually, most of it is valuable. Everything, that is, except school carpool lines and late-night conference calls. It's hard to imagine giving any of it up because most of us like to be busy, feel productive, and watch our kids play all the games.

What could we gain, though, with more time back in our schedules? The reality is that time is finite, and the pace of our lives directly impacts the quality of our relationship with Christ.

When we have crammed schedules and are so busy getting from point A to point B and keeping track of everything in between, we get stressed, anxious, overwhelmed, and eventually burnt out. We have no room for anyone or anything else, let alone Jesus. Even if we have time to squeeze Him in, it will likely be with a short-form devotional.

For many of us, our time with God dwindled so slowly over time that we hardly realized it happened, to the point where our fast-paced, get-it-done schedule has filled up all the time we used to devote to Him.

To intentionally parent our kids to stand firm in their faith in this culture, we must re-examine our pace. Not because our pace is bad in and of itself, but because it takes us away from Jesus and, often, our family. Intentionally raising our kids and fortifying them for the fire will take energy and time, which we will only have if we make changes.

Priorities – What we place the most value on in our lives

I remember, after my precious brother, Eric, was killed over a decade ago, having my first "aha" moment about priorities. While I had several life-altering realizations after that traumatic loss in my life, one of the most impactful ones was this: life is short. Tomorrow is not a given. That may sound somber and dark, but it's true. We live life believing we have more time. And yet, we don't. Many people know God has called them to something but haven't responded because of money, comfort, and time. We rationalize and say, "I'll do that when my house is paid off," or "When I have x amount in my 401K," or "When my kids are out of college." We delay God's call, believing we have time that we don't, because we fear giving up our comfort and security to do what God has asked. In the meantime, our stress levels are through the roof, we're rarely home, and when we are, we're preoccupied.

Many of us also don't venture to do what God has called us to because we struggle to believe that Scripture is true and that God is good. We believe that if we follow His call, we will lose everything. God does require sacrifice on this faith journey, and sometimes it's a lot, but from personal experience, I can attest that our family has never gone without shelter, food, basketball sign-up fees, and kids' braces. God provides for all of it because He knows what we need and even cares about what we want. He is a good Father.

God's desires for us and our family are good, too. They are even better than our own. He's the one who made us and knows what He made us for and what He made us to do. He gave us our talents, gifts, and passions, and He will use them for His glory and our good if we let Him. He won't leave us out in the cold in the process.

Scripture does not tell us to hustle, strive, make things happen, climb the corporate ladder, and focus on material wealth. The biblical worldview speaks to a different way of living that focuses on trust, dependence, surrender, and obedience. In a nutshell, faith — a faith that remembers our Lord owns the cattle on a thousand hills; reminds us not to worry about what we will eat, drink, or wear; and says God knows what we need before we even know we need it.

Re-evaluating where we are in life, where we are going, and whether we've asked God to guide us in the process is essential to raising Christian kids. When we follow God's direction for our lives, we have more time with our family, more space in our life and calm in our spirit, and our kids will witness what it means to follow after Christ in complete trust and dependence, not superficial belief.

Perspective – How we view our lives and training up our kids

As we can imagine, our kids' perspective of this world differs significantly from ours. It's not that they don't experience the same things we did, like the desire for acceptance, the discomfort with who we are, the need to break free of our parents as we tried to find our way, or even those awkward teenage years and bad acne. What's different about our kids' experience today is three-fold: a world that now believes boys can become girls, immediate access to information on any number of topics and devices, and added to that, a lack of biblical understanding.

In other words, we have a changing postmodern culture that tells our kids to disregard truth; we have a social media matrix that serves up various and, at times, insidious information to our kids void of truth, and our kids don't have a firm foundation and understanding of truth to decipher the biblical truth from the lies. Additionally, many of our kids' faith may not be their own yet.

So, what are we to do?

We shift our perspective and equip our kids with the knowledge of Scripture and the ideologies of this world so they can discern the two. We won't be there for every question they have, but we can equip them to stand firm in their faith in this increasingly confusing culture through this five-point framework: Personal Relationship with Christ & Purpose, Theology, Culture & Worldview, Apologetics, and Critical Thinking Skills.

1. Personal Relationship & Purpose

It's not uncommon for us to want to skip our kids right past their personal relationship with Christ and send them straight into an apologetics class. However, it's so important that our kids have a relationship with Christ and genuine faith before we ask them to defend it, because then our kids will speak empty words from a place of knowledge versus true transformative faith. Encouraging our kids to pray, read the Bible, listen to worship music, and attend church each week develops critical spiritual disciplines that will impact their spiritual growth.

One of the most important things we can do is speak to our kids about their God-given purpose. God has plans for each of us and our kids, and speaking that into our kids' lives is so valuable. The main reason some kids fall into social justice activism is because it gives them meaning and purpose to effect change through their posts, reels, and protests. Our kids need to find that same sense of purpose in Christ.

A powerful way to communicate God's purpose to our children is by reminding them that God will use their gifts, passions, and experiences to bring His plans to pass through their lives to build His Kingdom. Praying together for God's purpose in their lives effectively keeps them inspired and excited about God's plans.

2. Theology

Part of our kids' personal relationship with and purpose in Christ is understanding what they believe. Equipping our kids with solid theology is essential. Theology is the study of God through the Bible. Learning theology helps us grasp the core beliefs of our faith and the major themes we find in Scripture. Theology also gives our children a solid biblical worldview to process all the information they see and experience.

The lack of biblical understanding, or literacy, has led to many false beliefs in the Church, including the latest movement to infiltrate the Church, called progressive "Christianity," which we will cover in a future chapter.

3. Culture & Worldview

Once our kids have a solid grasp of their faith and theology, teaching them about culture and worldview will prepare them for the world. To discern truth from lies, they have to know the truth first, which is why theology is so important, and then secondly, they have to understand our culture's beliefs.

Part of comprehending culture is understanding people's different worldviews so our children can identify belief systems appropriately. Christianity is part of the theistic worldview, social justice warriorism is part of the postmodern worldview, and atheism is part of the naturalism worldview. This example highlights how our core belief systems link to a worldview.

4. Apologetics

The priority of these last two equipping musts is interchangeable, but both are essential. Apologetics is the skill of learning to defend the faith. It's understanding the common arguments against Christianity and then providing a reasoned response based on Scripture and sometimes science, which affirms our faith, not undermines it. With postmodernism as the prevailing worldview in our culture, the focus of apologetics is quickly changing because we must now defend our faith against new arguments. Not to mention the fact that those who believe in other worldviews are also actively creating apologetics to defend their beliefs against Christianity.

5. Critical Thinking Skills

This skill is often lost in our culture nowadays, which bases much of its decision making on emotion versus logic. Critical thinking skills allow us to look at core ideas and reason logically or critically about them. While generally a lost art today, this ability alone will help our kids rationally approach ideas with a brand-new lens that will lead them to a more reasonable conclusion.

This is how we equip our kids. It's also why we must re-evaluate our pace, priorities, and perspective to make room in our lives to prepare our kids to stand in the world and to stand against the enemy, who seeks to kill, steal, and destroy this Christian faith. It will require returning to what is essential in life: the King and the Kingdom, our family, and our faith.

A New Lens

If Oxford had a word of the year for Christian circles, “worldview” would win. Like many, I had never heard of “worldview” before 2020. The word grew in popularity as many Christian thinkers began articulating more concisely what was happening in the world and, more specifically, what was going wrong.

A worldview is the lens through which we see the world and how we perceive it. Most of us have not considered our worldview. We may even have a “whirled-view,” as John Stonestreet would call it, “made up of a smorgasbord of contradictory, but personally satisfying and culturally popular ideas.”[5] Whatever our worldview is, it impacts all areas of our lives, even if we’ve never thought about it.

One of the most effective tools to equip our children with is the ability to decipher worldviews, which can start at a young age. Right now, the number of ideas that bombard our kids daily is like a plate of spaghetti: interwoven so we can't determine where one idea begins and another ends. The ideas all get tangled up together.

To properly untangle the confusing messages our kids hear regularly, we need a system to categorize them effectively. This way, we untangle the mess, make sense of it, and determine whether the ideas align with our beliefs.

For example, one of the easiest ways for our kids to spot the difference between a biblical worldview and a postmodern worldview is through the topic of evil. Most specifically, what constitutes evil and who perpetrates it.

In a worldview and apologetics class I was leading with a group of middle and high schoolers at our church, we discussed the issue of evil. I asked them to list what they considered evil, and here's what they shared:

- Blasphemy
- Lying
- Murder
- Greed
- Pride
- Sexual immorality
- Abortion
- Injustice
- Jealousy
- Cheating
- Idolatry
- Hate
- Distractions from God
- Dishonoring your father and mother (I may have added that one!)

Their ideas about evil expressly come from a biblical worldview.

They know what God called evil in His Word, and so that's how these students defined evil. This example describes what a worldview does. It impacts how we view the world, and not just some aspects; a worldview impacts how we see everything.

For the postmodern worldview, the problem of evil is very different. It's less broad ranging than the biblical view and centers on the core ideas of injustice and oppression.

A worldview goes beyond what we think about evil, too, and it impacts how we think about meaning, purpose, work, death, goodness, morality, authority, social causes, and more. Much of it comes down to answering these worldview questions found in *How Now Shall We Live?* by Chuck Colson and Nancy Pearcey:[6]

1. Where did we come from, and who are we?
2. What has gone wrong with the world?
3. What can we do to fix the world?
4. How should we live in light of all this?

Our worldview goes beyond these broader intellectual topics and affects our everyday lives. It impacts everything we do, like how we react to sin in our lives, love other people, handle conflict, spend our time and money, and raise our children.

I heard two kids playing a video game once, and one expressed hatred toward another player who had killed this child's avatar. The friend, also playing the game, stopped and said, "You can't hate him. The Bible says to forgive one another as God forgave us." I loved hearing that exchange because it undoubtedly expressed a biblical worldview. The friend got their idea about handling conflict directly from the Bible. That was this child's worldview showing up in real life.

If you searched how many worldviews exist, you would get responses ranging from four to eight. We can sum up the most prevailing belief systems in our world today by focusing on the four outlined in the book *Making Sense of Your World* by W. Gary Phillips, William E. Brown, and John Stonestreet[7], which are naturalism, transcendentalism, theism, and postmodernism.

To make it easier for our kids to understand and articulate, I've given each worldview an easy-to-remember nickname starting with S.

1. The Science Worldview (Naturalism)

Whether through a microscope or a telescope, this worldview is about what we can physically see. Think stars and galaxies, trees and mountains, or the human cell and DNA. Whether vast or nanosized, if we can see it, it's real, according to this worldview.

The science worldview, or naturalism, based solely on logical thought and reason, excludes any possibility of a spiritual world or supernatural being. Believers of this worldview are, by definition, atheists since they don't believe in God or even the chance there could be one.

For this worldview, science is the god or the religion. If science comes up with a theory about the origins of life, like evolution, then followers of this worldview will believe it. Since this worldview focuses on the natural world of what is visible, it becomes more understandable why proponents of this worldview focus on the earth, oceans, and climate. Because, in this belief system, the earth is the most important thing. It is life and the only reason life exists.

2. The Spiritual Worldview (Transcendentalism)

In many ways, this worldview is the exact opposite of the science worldview. Instead of logic and reason, it focuses on emotions, feelings, and the inner self. The supernatural is more real than the natural, and life is a journey to figure out that enlightened path.

In the spiritual worldview, or transcendentalism, everything's connected, like people, animals, and nature. It's one extensive universal network where all of us are one. The universe is supreme and often thought of like God, so thanking the universe has become en vogue. Energy, vibrations, and manifestations are popular vernacular, especially for New Agers.

Self-realization is king, and divinity is within. Just look inside yourself, empty your mind, and the answers will appear. Eternity happens through reincarnation, and the purpose of life is to constantly evolve spiritually in the natural world to reach more spiritual awareness.

Followers of this worldview activate around animal rights because of the oneness found in nature, humans, and animals. Religious beliefs in this worldview are Buddhism, Hinduism, New Age, and Native American.

3. The Submitted Worldview (Theism)

The worldview of Christians, Jews, and Muslims falls into the submitted worldview, or theism. This worldview hinges on the belief that there is a God who is personal and accessible, created the world, and fashioned humankind as finite beings who had a beginning and did not evolve.

God has authority over all, and our role is to obey and worship Him. In this worldview, people only live once, and God's judgment determines each person's eternity at death. Followers of this worldview believe in both the supernatural and the natural, the invisible and the visible.

Since this worldview holds that God is the Creator of human life, the typical social cause of this belief system is human rights. It is why, for example, Christians have always been at the forefront of human rights issues like abortion and sex trafficking.

4. Social Justice Worldview (Postmodernism)

The most recent worldview to enter the world stage and shake us to the core is the social justice worldview, or postmodernism. In this worldview, truth does not have an objective standard (i.e., true for everyone) because each person determines their own truth based on their culture, family dynamic, religion, socioeconomic status, and where they grew up.

This worldview hyper-focuses on injustice and the power structures perceived in society. In this belief system, the world consists of those in power (the oppressors) and those who do not have power (the oppressed). Those in power are the ones who constructed, or built up, society in a certain way, known as social constructs. The only way to overturn those power structures and social constructs (think gender and the justice system) is to deconstruct, or tear down, society. In other words, to break down the systems created by power structures, typically considered to be the patriarchy.

This worldview's concern is exclusively with what it considers minority or marginalized communities spanning ethnicity, LGBTQ+, women, disabled, and socioeconomically disadvantaged.

They rally around issues surrounding these communities, like abortion and LGBTQ+ rights.

Practically Understanding Worldview

Understanding these four worldviews will drastically increase your child's ability to discern the truth of God's Word from the lies they find in the world. One way to cement these ideas in your child's mind is to help them compare and contrast ideas they see in society.

I recently took a group of teen girls through an exercise of determining if the memes (messages) in their social feeds align with biblical beliefs, an idea I got from Kathy Gibbens of the *Filter It Through a Brain Cell* podcast. This exercise is an incredibly effective way to teach kids to evaluate the messages they hear and categorize them appropriately. An exercise like this develops critical thinking skills. Rather than taking every message at face value, our kids can bounce an idea off a standard foundation for what they know is true from Scripture and decide if it aligns with their beliefs.

Critical thinking skills form when there is a foundation of truth to compare ideas against. Understanding the biblical worldview, that is, the truth found in Scripture, will solidify truth in our kids' minds. They can then discern whether the ideas they hear in the world agree with the biblical worldview. So, that's what is up next ... understanding the biblical worldview.

> *Do not conform any longer to the pattern of this world, but be transformed by the renewing of your mind. Then you will be able to test and approve what God's will is—his good, pleasing and perfect will* (Romans 12:2).

5

A Biblical Worldview

I remember the first time I heard the gospel explained using the whole of Scripture from Genesis 1 to Revelation 22. My brain exploded like that little mind-blown emoji. I had no idea why or how I had never heard the gospel quite like that. Even the idea that the gospel encapsulated more than just two parts, starting in Genesis 3 with the Fall and ending in the Gospels of Matthew, Mark, Luke, and John with the death, burial, and Resurrection of Jesus, was like a foreign concept to me. Especially given that's what my evangelism training had taught me.

But here I sat in my monthly cohort meeting as part of the Colson Center for Christian Worldview intensive program I had signed up for, hearing about how the gospel includes four parts, which starts at the wondrous creation in Genesis 1, moves to the treacherous Fall, crescendos with the beauty of Jesus' redemption, and majestically ends at restoration when Jesus returns, all of which Chuck Colson and Nancy Pearcey outline in the book *How Now Shall We Live?* [8]

These four "chapters" of the gospel comprise the biblical worldview, which takes root in Scripture and comes from a foundational theology (study) of God's Word. There are important implications, too, for teaching our kids the gospel in these four parts instead of two, mainly because of our culture's, and subsequently our children's, obsession with identity, meaning, and purpose.

Let me explain.

Today, the world is screaming at our kids to be authentic, be their true selves, write their own stories, and be who they "really" are or who they want to be. There is an obsession with authenticity, to stop bending to the rules of the world (that is, the patriarchy), and to discover their authentic identity, with endless options for who or what that identity could be. Our kids are no longer considering whether to be a doctor or a lawyer when they grow up, but rather if they want to be a he, she, or they.

A friend of mine whose child identifies as the opposite gender and who has spent countless hours understanding trans ideology, described it like this, "Being your authentic self in today's society is being anything other than who you are. If you see yourself as who you are, then proponents of this ideology will convince you that you're being inauthentic to your true self."

What a warped sense of self our kids will hear throughout their lifetime. It's a view that creates chaos and confusion, and intentionally so. It's the reason God gave us the word "genuine" for our ministry. The culture is shouting "authenticity," and the root word *auth* comes from the word "author," meaning to write your own story. The word "authenticity" takes root in the idea of self, looking to self, searching self, and idolizing self to determine our destiny.

The word *gen* shares its root with words like genesis, generations, genius, genealogy, genitals, gender, and genetics. That Latin root word is about our birth/origin and that which produces. *Genuine* itself in Latin means "originating from the one true source." It's the real, true nature of. Hence, Genuine Family Ministries signals the actual true nature of the family. It is what the One true source had in mind when He created the beauty of the family, which consists of individuals made in the image of God.

That's what we find in Genesis 1 — the real, true nature of God's creation, including male and female — and that's why it's so critical that we start our gospel understanding and teaching to our kids here. The first part of the good news story is that we have a Creator who created us and the universe with intention, purpose, and meaning, and our identity is in Him.

This biblical idea of our identity is contrary to the world's idea, which would have us believe our sense of self, or identity, is in our sexuality, feelings, skin tone, ability, or socioeconomic status. For this reason, starting in Genesis for our gospel story is essential in today's culture.

In a society where identity has become the central theme, our kids must know where their identity comes from: the Creator, not the self. The One who designed us knows what He designed us for, and we go to Him and His Word for the answer.

Genesis 1 answers our first worldview question from Chapter 4, "Where did we come from, and who are we?"

Part 1: Creation (and Our Identity)

In the beginning, God created everything, including humankind, and it was good. The phrase "it was good" in Hebrew means that it worked as designed. Before that, when God first commanded, "Let there be light" in the darkness, the word "light" in Hebrew means order, which means that in the beginning, God created order in the chaos, and it worked as He had intended it to work.

God explains that He created us in His image, and what He created was very good. *"So God created man in his own image, in the image of God he created him; male and female he created them"* (Genesis 1:27). This is where our identity comes from, so what exactly does it mean?

- For starters, it means we all have inherent value and worth. God reminds us in Genesis 9:6 that we are not to kill another human because everyone is made in His image.
- Secondly, it means we inherit some of God's characteristics — not all of them, like omniscience or omnipotence, but some, like the ability to reason, understand morality, require justice, create beauty, speak to and relate to God on a spiritual level, be compassionate, or even get angry.
- Lastly, it means that we are representatives of God here on earth as God's image bearers. John Piper says this: "For us as image bearers it is to image (reflect) who God is, how great He is, and what He's like. We live in a way, think in a way, we feel in a way, we speak in a way that calls attention to the brightness of the glory of God."[9]

In this first chapter of Scripture, we also find our purpose. God tells Adam and Eve in Genesis 1:28, *"Be fruitful and increase in number; fill the earth and subdue it."* In other words, "Make more image bearers of me – just like you are image bearers." This command is symmetrical to the Great Commission in Matthew 28:19 to "go therefore and make disciples of all nations." It's the idea of being fruitful, multiplying, and making more of something.

The subtle phrase "and subdue it" means to bring the earth under authority. Chuck Colson called this "The Cultural Commission"[10] and likened it in importance to the Great Commission. It means that our responsibility as image bearers of God is to act as salt and light in our culture, to share our faith, and to represent Christ in our society, including through institutions like education and business. We do that through the work God plans for us, unique to each person.

In the beginning, everything was pure and perfect; sin had not entered the world and defiled our hearts. Better yet, God's presence was visible, and our relationship with Him was personal and accessible. We understood God as our Creator and our role in His Kingdom.

This is part one of our gospel story.

Part 2: The Fall

In Genesis 3, disorder became part of human existence when sin entered the world. Sin, or disobedience to God's ordered plan, created dysfunction, and the world was no longer working as God designed.

When that happened, sin broke four primary relationships, evident in Genesis 3 through the curses, including:

- Our relationship with self. We now have death and suffering.
- Our relationship with others. We now have conflict with people.

- Our relationship with creation. The earth is now cursed.
- Our relationship with God. God separates us from His presence.

Practically speaking, the effects of sin appear in our lives in several ways. One is through spiritual warfare, such as Paul talked about when he said in Ephesians 6:12, *"For our struggle is not against flesh and blood, but against the rulers, against the authorities ... against the spiritual forces of evil in the heavenly realms."* Another way is through personal disobedience as part of our sinful nature when we engage in greed, pride, lying, stealing, idolatry, sexual immorality, and more. Additionally, we live in a broken world affected by sin that creates suffering, such as disease and death. While the latter is often not a result of personal sin, it is a result of sin in the world. So, in short, sin shows up in our lives through Satan, self, and suffering.

Sin harms and has consequences for ourselves, others, and our relationship with Christ. It creates spiritual separation from God, our Creator. As John Piper says, "When the Fall happened, our image in God was not destroyed, but it was defaced."[11] We are still made in His image, blessed to do the work He calls us to, but the world changed for the worse when sin entered it, making it a daily challenge for us all.

The existence of evil, including what causes it, who perpetrates it, and what comprises it, is just as important to the biblical worldview as how God created us and restores all that evil destroys. Sin, or disobedience to God's commands, answers our second worldview question, "What has gone wrong with the world?"

Part 3: Redemption

Part three of our gospel story is redemption, which is how God sovereignly orchestrated the reconciliation of humankind back to Himself after sin created separation.

God accomplished this through the Savior, Jesus Christ. Redemption answers the third worldview question, "What can we do to fix our world?"

Before Jesus came to earth, priests facilitated the forgiveness of sins for individuals through the animal sacrifices they offered. If the offering was to cover sin, it required a blood sacrifice from a blemish-free animal, one without defect, pure and perfect. This sacrifice included the burnt offering to cover sins, the sin offering to cover sins unknowingly committed, and the guilt offering to cover unintentional sins.

In this system, the person brought the sacrifice to the priest to receive atonement and forgiveness for sins. Leviticus 4:31 says, *"In this way the priest will make atonement for him, and he will be forgiven."* The priest acted as a mediator between God and man, but only God has the authority to forgive sins.

God explained why the blood sacrifice is necessary in Leviticus 17:11, *"For the life of a creature is in the blood, and I have given it to you to make atonement for yourselves on the altar; it is the blood that makes atonement for one's life."* Again, in Hebrews 9:22, it says that *"without the shedding of blood there is no forgiveness."*

Even in the Garden, God covered Adam and Eve. Genesis 3:21 says, *"The Lord God made garments of skin for Adam and his wife and clothed them."* To make garments of skin, an animal sacrifice and the shedding of blood was necessary. Since the beginning, God's justice was on display, making right what sin made wrong.

Romans 5 says, in short, that just like sin entered the world through one man, Adam, salvation is available through one man, Jesus. We also learn in Hebrews 4:14–15 that Jesus is now our High Priest *"who has been tempted in every way, just as we are — yet he did not sin."*

Jesus alone can atone for all our sins because He is the Son of God. He is divine; He is God. Jesus said so, God said so, the disciples knew it, and the demons did, too. Jesus' birth, Resurrection, and ascension into heaven were each miraculous. In the life of Jesus, God supernaturally orchestrated events to atone for our sins and offer redemption by paying the price we should have paid ourselves.

Born of a virgin, Jesus lived a sinless (pure, blemish-free) life, which God required — Jesus' whole life was a preparation to be the sacrifice for our sins to heal a broken world. Now, instead of atonement for sins by the regular offering of animal sacrifices, Jesus became the final sacrificial lamb, and His blood covers the sins of those who believe.

Before Jesus' death, the high priest was the only one permitted in the Holy of Holies, the most sacred place in the temple, separated by a thick curtain, where God's Spirit dwelled. When Jesus died, Scripture explains in Matthew 27:51, *"At that moment the curtain of the temple was torn in two from top to bottom,"* symbolizing that we now have direct access to God through Jesus' blood sacrifice for all believers.

John 3:16 tells us, *"For God so loved the world that he gave his one and only Son, that whoever believes in him shall not perish but have eternal life."* And Romans 3:23-25 states, *"for all have sinned and fall short of the glory of God, and all are justified freely by his grace through the redemption that came by Christ Jesus. God presented Christ as a sacrifice of atonement, through the shedding of his blood."*

In Christ's death, burial, and Resurrection, God heals our relationship with Him by forgiving our sins. No matter what we've done in this world, we can turn (repent) to God and ask for forgiveness, and He is faithful to forgive. Jesus saves, and His forgiveness heals.

We also see the image of God at work here, too. Jesus is the perfect image of God; He lived a sinless life and shows us what it takes to follow Him. So, while we are made in the image of God, Jesus is the *"image of the invisible God"* (Colossians 1:15).

Part three of our gospel explains that our world gets fixed by God's forgiveness of our sins through Jesus' death on the Cross for all who believe.

Part 4: Restoration (and Our Purpose)

Part four of our gospel story is restoration, when Jesus returns and makes everything new. It's when final restoration occurs, and the four relationships that sin broke are healed. This part answers our fourth worldview question, "How do we live in light of all this?"

We live in the time period between when Christ came and when Christ will come again. Our hope is in this future restoration when we reside with God for eternity and when there is no more brokenness or pain. Revelation 21:3–5 says, "*'Now the dwelling of God is with men, and he will live with them. They will be his people, and God himself will be with them and be their God. He will wipe every tear from their eyes. There will be no more death or mourning or crying or pain, for the old order of things has passed away.' He who was seated on the throne said, 'I am making everything new!'*"

We have work to do between now and when Jesus returns. The restoration part of our gospel reminds us that we have purpose and meaning in our lives and that what we do on this earth matters for the Kingdom of God.

We also must get back to a clearer view of the image of God. When Christ came, He gave us a perfect example of what it means to live in the image of God. We are now to reflect the character of Christ, and we have the Holy Spirit to help us. "... *[S}ince you have taken off your old self with its practices and have put on the new self, which is being renewed in knowledge in the image of its Creator*" (Colossians 3:9–10).

In this phase, between part three (redemption) and part four (restoration) of our gospel story, before Jesus returns, we must focus on transforming into the image of God and on the purpose God calls us to. Sanctification describes this transformation process by the Holy Spirit, and as this process unfolds in our lives, the fruits of the Spirit become evident. This is how we demonstrate to a dark and dying world the beauty and the light of the salvation we've received and the Lord we follow.

The Language of the Biblical Worldview

Articulating the biblical worldview in these four parts rather than two will help our children understand their identity and purpose in Christ and protect them from popular postmodern ideas. Additionally, as with all worldviews, the biblical worldview has a vocabulary our kids need to know and understand. To sum up what Shane Pruitt says, if our kids can understand algebra, chemistry, geometry, biology, and physics, they can understand our Christian faith.

Here are a few essential terms to teach them:	
Sin	Disobedience to God's Word/commands
Original sin	The belief that we all have inherited a sinful nature since birth, based on the first sin of Adam and Eve
Salvation	The saving of humans from sin (and the eternal consequences of sin) through faith in Jesus Christ as Lord and Savior
Atonement	The forgiveness, or covering, of our sins through Jesus' blood sacrifice
Justification	Made righteous (holy, without sin) before the Lord
Reconciliation	Reuniting with God as a result of atonement and faith
Sanctification	The process of transforming into the image of Christ by the work of the Holy Spirit in our lives to purify us

Teaching our kids the vernacular of the faith equips them as they study Scripture because these words are frequent in the New Testament. Understanding God's Word can be challenging if we don't know the meaning of specific terms.

Our gospel is robust, and while simple, it does require context and understanding to ensure our faith is true, which is why we cannot minimize it. The Holy Spirit can indeed move and instantly change hearts, but in our Christian culture, we have often minimized the gospel to move people quickly to Christ rather than take the time to disciple. Jesus instructed us to disciple people as part of the Great Commission because discipleship gives us the firm foundation of our faith, not a commoditized gospel. Jesus even warns us of the implications of a faith not rooted in understanding in Matthew 13:18–23. Specifically, verse 23 states, "*But the seed falling on good soil refers to someone* who hears the word and understands it. *This is the one who produces a crop, yielding a hundred, sixty or thirty times what was sown*" (emphasis mine).

Ensuring our kids have a comprehensive view of the gospel is essential because our lack of biblical understanding as a Church has allowed false beliefs to seep into our congregations. Our best defense against the ideas of this world is to know God's Word first and foremost and then to understand the ideas that come against it, which is where we are heading next in Chapter 6.

6

A Contemporary *Apologetic*

I've heard it said that while the gospel never changes, apologetics do because the central purpose of an apologetic, or defense of the faith as the Greek word *apologia* translates, is to defend the gospel in the current culture (aka society).

The word *apologia* appears in the Bible several times, translated as "give an answer" in 1 Peter 3:15, *"Always be prepared to give an answer to everyone who asks you to give the reason for the hope that you have. But do this with gentleness and respect."*

To give a response, defense, or a reason for our hope in Christ is what apologetics means. We may even think of apologetics as an argument for the faith. With phrases like "defense of" and "arguments for," it's easy to understand why apologetics can sometimes get a bad rap, especially when approached with a defensive or win-the-argument-at-all-costs attitude. That's why Peter clearly says, "*But do this with gentleness and respect.*" The posture of our heart, sharing the truth with love, must always be how we approach conversations of the faith.

Paul also spoke of the concept of apologetics when he said, "*To the Jews I became like a Jew, to win the Jews. To those under the law I became like one under the law ... so as to win those under the law. ... To the weak I became weak, to win the weak. I have become all things to all men so that by all possible means I might save some. I do all this for the sake of the gospel ...*" (1 Corinthians 9:20–23).

To defend the faith, we must know what we are defending it against, which is what Paul describes. We need to understand today's ideas, the background and framework for what people believe (their worldview), to formulate a biblical response. Apologetics is not only for unbelievers who deny Christianity; it also helps to defend against false teachings in the Church and to teach our children.

The apologetics we most commonly learn about are the existence of God, the accuracy of Scripture, responses to other religions, and creation versus evolution. These apologetics continue to be extremely important as we dig into deeper theological and scientific conversations for those who deny the validity of the Christian faith. Mostly, they are beneficial in conversations based on reason and logic.

What do we do, however, when we are no longer talking about intellect and instead are talking about emotions? How do we respond when the cause of the century is injustice and the motivating power behind it is "love"? What can we do when those two basic elements – injustice and love – sound oddly like a new gospel, or as Paul called it, "Another Gospel"?

New thoughts require new apologetics, and this is where we find ourselves today, embarking on a new world of ideas inside and outside the Church, such as:

- Truth is not the same for everyone, making it nonexistent.
- To discover one's authentic self, one must explore their gender and sexual identity.
- Just love and don't judge.
- God is love, and that is His only quality.
- Jesus was a social justice warrior.
- The patriarchy wrote all history, including the Bible, so we can't trust it.

These ideas stem from the postmodern worldview and, in some cases, have infiltrated Christian thought. To understand where we are in our culture and churches, we must review the formation of the postmodern/critical theory worldview and its foundational elements.

The Postmodern Worldview

Postmodernism and critical theory started as separate ideas, and there's debate on which influenced society first. Postmodernism in and of itself is the rejection of the modern era of reason, logic, and science. It's the birth of the subjective, feelings-based, anti-truth movement. If you search for it online, you may find more references to art than to worldview.

Over twenty years ago, in a college class for my literary studies degree, the professor asked us what the book we were reading meant to each of us individually. He explained that it didn't matter what the author intended; what mattered was how we interpreted it in light of our lives. This new way of teaching the arts disregarded the creator's intent and expressed much of what we see in the postmodern era today: a focus on self as the primary, most important character in the story, with our lived experiences as our narrative.

According to Neil Shenvi, critical theory first came to be when a group of sociologists and philosophers attended the Frankfurt School in Frankfurt, Germany, in the early 1920s, critiquing how people in power influenced societies.[12] It was an evolution of Karl Marx's cultural critique of capitalism.

From a critical theory perspective, justice occurs when equity (equal outcomes), not equality (equal opportunities), exists. Institutions that create injustice are the problem; the solution is deconstruction, or the tearing down, of these institutions. This critical theory framework gets applied to all perceived minority causes spanning gender, ethnicity, sexuality, economic class, (dis) ability, and more.

Postmodernism appeared in the art world in the 1950s before becoming a prominent social thought, but neither postmodernism nor critical theory gained steam until the 1970s or so. From my perspective, postmodernism and critical theory form the postmodern worldview we see today. Without critical theory, postmodernism wouldn't have much substance or a framework to lean on and activate around. Without postmodernism, critical theory would have had to contend with objective (unchangeable) truth, making it nearly impossible to push concepts like gender fluidity.

As of today, they mesh together, making a complete story out of two halves. So, while they are technically two movements that have been around for over eighty years each, I consider them the foundation of the postmodern worldview for the sake of this conversation.

Foundational Elements of Postmodernism

Reviewing the terminology associated with the postmodern worldview will help us best understand the worldview. The vocabulary explains who is involved, the problem, how we can view it, the solution, and who creates it. It will answer our worldview questions of what went wrong with the world and how we fix it.

Who is involved?

Oppressed	The people in society who do not have power and have suffered accordingly. For example, people of color (POC) or those in the LGBTQ+ lifestyle.
Oppressors	People who have power in society, typically referring to the patriarchy.
Patriarchy	Old, rich white men who institute or enable power structures in society.

What is the problem?

Social Constructs	The idea that the patriarchy constructed society to work in a specific way, resulting in the creation of institutions, like marriage, and conventions, such as the binary of male and female. As a result, some people have experienced injustice, which has led to the oppressed category.

How can we view the problem?

Truth	A person's experience determines their truth, including upbringing, family dynamics, religion, socioeconomic status, ethnicity, sexual and gender identity, and more. Any belief that objective (unchanging) truth exists has likely created a social construct.
Lived experience	The personal experience of someone in an oppressed category. Their understanding of that experience ultimately forms their truth.
Intersectionality	A term coined by Kimberle Crenshaw, this is the practice of looking at the intersection of race, gender, class (socioeconomic status), and (dis)ability to understand the compounding effects of being part of multiple minority or oppressed groups. It makes someone's voice or "lived experience" more credible and meaningful. For example, someone who is a person of color, gay, an immigrant, and disabled would fall into multiple oppressed categories and therefore has presumably experienced more injustice, making their perspective, or truth, more valuable. Additionally, it means that someone in an oppressed category can also be an oppressor, adding complexity to the dynamic.

What is the solution?

Deconstruction	Destroying or tearing down social constructs, including ideas and institutions, such as the justice system.
Equity	Equal outcomes, not equal opportunities, for minority groups. Equity guarantees oppressed groups the same outcomes (rewards or jobs) to balance the scoreboard or to overcorrect it in light of past injustices.

Who or what can help?

Social justice warriors	People who activate around the social justice causes of race, gender, and sexuality.
Allies	People who align themselves with people in the oppressed categories and champion social justice causes. Allies are not typically part of the oppressed categories they support.
Diversity, Equity, and Inclusion (DEI)	Programs, typically introduced in businesses, government, and other organizations, meant to create equity and elevate oppressed voices as equal, or in most cases, more important than those who fall into oppressor categories

These definitions explain postmodern ideology and the course correction it deems necessary to create a good and moral society. According to critical theory, deconstruction is ultimately the solution to create equity. With this in mind, we must understand the power of deconstruction and its influence on our culture when used to create social justice change.

This critical theory framework also applies to the critical theory disciplines of gender, sexuality, and race. In future chapters, we will discover how this framework affects our culture through feminism, sex positivity, gender and sexual identity, race, and its impact on the Church and how we can equip our kids in light of this.

The Power of Deconstruction to Make Change

As part of the postmodern worldview, deconstructing core ideas and institutions means breaking them down, reimagining what they should be, and then reconstructing them in a new way, which is necessary to make any notable changes to society. That's the essence of deconstruction. It targets our most sacred beliefs as Christ followers, including the binary of male and female, marriage between one man and one woman, the sanctity and purpose of life and family, and the very Christian faith where we put our trust. More than anything else, I estimate that this post-modern movement is not only intent on destroying the family and the gender binary, but on destroying Christianity.

It's safe to say that the deconstruction playbook works something like this: Cause confusion and chaos, Change the narrative, and Create activists.

1. Cause Confusion & Chaos

The confusion and chaos are evident in the conversation around gender and sexual identity. Consider this: Before the LGBTQ+ movement, it was the LGB (lesbian, gay, bisexual) movement, focused on making their sexual preferences and experiences normal, not shameful, and receiving equal rights and protections. In other words, the movement was for people who experienced same-sex attraction. Next came the T (transgender), which had to do with gender, not sexuality, when a person believed their gender identity was different than their biological sex. This condition, called gender dysphoria, is a psychological term noted in the DSM-5, which is a manual on mental disorders. Sexuality and gender are fundamentally different issues that have merged as one topic.

From there came the Q+ (queer plus everything else), which can include sexuality, gender, or a combination of the two.

The merged movements have now expanded beyond normalizing these experiences or ensuring equal rights to creating confusion and chaos in our youth. It's no longer for people who genuinely feel out of alignment with God's design (as an example, clinical gender dysphoria is pretty rare). Gender and sexuality are now up for grabs as a reconstruction of who you believe you are, who you want to be, and what experiences you want to have. The pressure on today's youth to examine every thought, feeling, and experience to determine where they fit into the gender identity matrix is real. Not only that, but our children will no longer receive resistance to their chosen identities from their peers, but rather a celebration and an undercurrent of acceptance and approval that teens have craved since the dawn of time.

2. Change the Narrative

With the new common language of critical theory comes an opportunity to change or create a new narrative to rally people. Not only do we have new words and phrases like intersectionality, social construct, and allies, but also the redefining of already defined words. In Hillary Ferrer's book *Mama Bear Apologetics*, she refers to this phenomenon as linguistic theft.[13] The redefining of words further creates confusion and establishes this new narrative. Many instances of this exist, but a few main redefined words are:

Truth	There is no absolute truth. I can determine my own.
Identity	Self-defined and fluid.
Love	Defined as embracing someone's identity.
Morality	Demonstrating love toward everyone (see definition of love).
Purpose	To defend these worldview ideas.

I heard a quote once that said something like this, "I can think of nothing more important to fight over than words." Words move people. They tell a story, become familiar, explain our experiences in life, and create a common way for us to think. It's why Christians have our own language (e.g., sin, salvation, reconciliation) and other worldviews have their own, too.

3. Create Activists

To create a movement, there must be people who passionately power the movement. That's what this cause is so effective at doing, primarily because they have no shortage of stories of injustice to tell or to invent. By "invent," I simply mean that because they tell a story, they essentially create the narrative around the oppressor and the oppressed, or the victimizer and the victim. Consider abortion, for example. Feminist activists are so vocal about their bodies and reproductive rights and the career or life experiences they wouldn't have if they had that child they never wanted. It's easy for a young girl to imagine herself as the main character of that story and decide that she, too, wouldn't want an unwanted pregnancy to tie her down and "ruin her life." Thus, an activist is born, even if she's never considered having sex.

These groups also understand the value of coming together and uniting around a cause. They recognize that, whether they champion race, women, or LGBTQ+ causes, they can see more advancement for their cause together than if operating separately. There is strength in numbers, which is why we saw the joining of the LGB with the TQ+ in more recent years. It's also why when you hear activists in these spaces speak, you will hear them say things like "race issues are women's issues" because they are forming a "one for all and all for one" mentality (that is, narrative).

Ibram X. Kendi, whom we will cover when we discuss critical race theory, has cornered the market on this idea of activism. He has a whole line of books about *How to Be an Antiracist* that he could have easily titled *How to Be an Activist* instead. He has a book for you and me to read, one for babies, one for young people, and one instructing parents on how to raise an antiracist. It's hard to blame him or any postmodern activists, though, because they are simply rallying around their cause, "their" truth, like we rally and evangelize around the real truth of God's Word.

So, what can we teach our kids? Since the deconstruction playbook is to confuse, change the narrative, and create activists, we must solidify our children's understanding of God's order, the biblical worldview, and their purpose in Christ. This becomes our new apologetic that defends against the ideas of today. In other words,

- Since the playbook is to confuse our kids, then we define God's design.
- Since the playbook is to change the narrative, then we orient our kids on God's narrative.
- Since the playbook is to create activists, then we raise Kingdom builders and disciple makers.

SEVEN PRINCIPLES OF GOD'S DESIGN

You can never start talking to your kids about God's design too early or too late. Talking about God's design is as vital as talking about the gospel because God's design and His character are foundational to the good news. He is the Creator. He is sovereign. He is the Rule Maker. He is just. He is love. His justice required the Cross, and His love sent His Son to it.

Grounding our kids' understanding of life through a biblical worldview starts with the foundational principles of God's design for how the world works and why we are here. These principles become our response, or defense, to the culture's narrative, that is, an apologetic. Share these seven concepts with your kids and reinforce them in conversations as they grow.

1. God is the Creator of the Universe

> *In the beginning God created the heavens and the earth* (Genesis 1:1).

If God is to have credibility in our kids' lives, they must understand why He has authority in our lives. God has authority because He is the sole reason we are alive, and He determines why we are here.

One of the most stunning proofs of God is His divine order for creation. He is the God of order and has a sequence for how His creation works. There are over 25 elements that must be fine-tuned for life to exist on earth. If one of these elements doesn't work precisely as designed, we will not survive. One example is the rate at which the universe is expanding. It makes for precisely the right conditions for life to exist. If the universe expanded even a bit faster, the heat and energy would dissipate too fast for life to be possible. If it expanded a bit slower, gravity would crush us. The fine-tuning is exquisite — 1 part to 10 to the 60th power — like one dollar out of a trillion, trillion, trillion, trillion, trillion dollars. The tolerance for error is minuscule.[14]

For the naturalist, or the science minded worldview that suggests we are here by a cosmic accident, there is too much proof of intentional design and creation to support a theory based on a mistake. Since God is the One who created us, He also knows how He created us and what He created us for, which leads to our following six principles.

2. God Made Us in His Image

> *Then God said, "Let us make man in our image, in our likeness ..."* (Genesis 1:26).

As shared in Chapter 5, being God's image bearers means that we have inherent value and worth, are granted some of His attributes, and we are to be representative of Him here on earth. Our feelings or emotions do not define our identity. God does.

3. God Designed the Binary of Male and Female

> *So God created man in his own image, in the image of God he created him; male and female he created them* (Genesis 1:27).

There is purposeful design in the binary of male and female. Without it, humankind would cease to exist because only a biological male and a biological female can produce a child. God made two distinct but complementary beings to create children. The body's design and the instinctual nature of males and females as fathers and mothers are what create healthy and thriving children.

Males and females have equal yet distinct purposes. When the man and woman come together in marriage, they become one flesh, both spiritually in the eyes of God and physically through the act of sex (Genesis 2:24).

Men and women as equal means they are both image bearers of God and given characteristics of God as a result. They have equal value and worth in God's eyes and His Kingdom. Men and women are also distinct in many ways, including spiritually, sexually, physically, emotionally, and mentally. We will discuss more of those differences in a future chapter so we can equip our kids.

Also, it's no mistake that I'm using the word "binary" to describe how God made us uniquely male and female. It's essential that, as parents, we use the term. Binary means two categories. In a world that's telling our kids there are no binaries (i.e., the term "nonbinary" identifies someone who doesn't see themselves in the categories of male or female), we need to teach our kids there is a binary when it comes to gender. Using this terminology reinforces that we are aware of modern-day language and ideas. It also teaches our kids how to respond to belief systems that suggest there is no binary.

4. Family Is Central to God's Design

> *God blessed them and said to them, "Be fruitful and increase in number; fill the earth and subdue it"* (Genesis 1:28).

God made it so that reproduction only occurs when one man and one woman come together in the act of sex. That child's survival is only possible through the nurturing, feeding, and caring of their parents. This demonstrates God's plan for the family. It's the only way to achieve our mandate in Genesis 1:28 to create more image bearers.

Family is the center of God's design. A healthy family is where we grow, teach, guide, and find joy and contentment. It's also where children find safety and security and how we preserve the Christian faith from generation to generation.

The parent and child relationship mirrors our relationship with God as our Father and us as His children. The Trinity is also a representation of the family. God Himself is three: Father, Son, and Holy Spirit. God reveals Himself to us as Father and Jesus as Son, which forms a parental structure. It's in His being, and He created it for us through the family structure.

5. God Created the Church

An essential extension of the family is the Church. It is the family of God, the Body of Christ, where the family grows in the knowledge of God. It's also where the Christian community comes together to grow in the Lord.

The Church is essential for Christian living and is where thriving in God's Word, giving back to the community, and sharing the good news all originate. In other words, the Church is the central hub for education on God's Word, edifying the Body of Christ through our spiritual gifts and evangelizing our communities and beyond with the good news of Jesus.

Jesus instituted the Church and said this in Matthew 16:18, *"And I tell you that you are Peter, and on this rock I will build my church, and the gates of Hades will not overcome it."* No matter what ideologies or people come against the Church, Jesus wins in the end, as does His Church.

We must share God's design and purpose for the Church with our children because when we talk about progressive "Christianity" in a future chapter, which is where the postmodern worldview meets Christianity, one of the main deconstruction ideas is to tear down the Church.

6. God Designed Us to Work

> *The Lord God took the man and put him in the Garden of Eden to work [cultivate] it and take care of it* (Genesis 2:15).

Work has been part of God's ordered design since the beginning of creation in Genesis. Even before Adam and Eve disobeyed God's instructions, God placed Adam in the Garden to work and "cultivate" it.

Adam was responsible for naming the animals and caring for, or watching over, the Garden. Part of Adam's purpose was his responsibility to God's creation through his work. It's the same for us.

Our identity, as made in the image of God, is evident through our natural tendency to work. God works, He creates, and we desire to work and create, too.

Culture comes from the word "cultivate," which refers to what we grow, build, and enhance in our world. Cultivating our "garden" should represent God and His design, with a dedication to His commands through our work. The more Christians do the work God calls us to, the less we will see the evil one running rampant, and the more we will see God's beauty, peace, and order abound in our world.

7. God Mandates Us to Restore Culture

> *God blessed them and said to them, "Be fruitful and increase in number; fill the earth and subdue it* (Genesis 1:28).

The cultural commission is about bringing our lives under God's reign and rule. To do this, we elevate God and His ways in our society through the work He planned for us to do. We will see a dramatic transformation in our communities and world when we are each doing the work He's purposed for us. The most prominent institutions in our culture need more Christ-centered believers to work, build, and cultivate for Christ.

God's Narrative

These seven principles provide a foundation for how we are to live and what we are to do. Our kids, now more than ever, need an understanding of their purpose and God's design. In addition to these principles, we can proactively teach our children the biblical definitions of specific words and how they differ from the previously shared postmodern definitions. This will help our children to understand the biblical worldview more clearly. It prepares them with a foundation of truth so they can more easily identify the lies of the postmodern worldview.

TRUTH – "I am the way, and the truth, and the life" (John 14:6).

Jesus tells us that He is the way, the truth, and the life, and that nobody comes to the Father except through Him. We find this truth in the Bible. It tells us everything we need to know about life, such as why we are here, what is evil, how to find restoration in a relationship with God, how to handle conflict, what roles to include in a church, how to follow Jesus, how to demonstrate our love to others, how to think about justice, what our priorities in life should be, how to think about money and work, how to treat our spouse, and how to train our children. That's not even a complete list. The list goes on and on because God gave us the guidebook of life and truth in the Bible and left us with the Holy Spirit as our guide into all truth (John 16:13).

IDENTITY – We are made in the Image of God (Genesis 1:27).

God bestowed the most incredible honor upon humankind by making us in His image. Even the angels and animals did not receive this privilege.

Scripture says in Psalm 139:13–14, *"For you created my inmost being; you knit me together in my mother's womb. I praise you because I am fearfully and wonderfully made ..."* We are so precious to God that He designs us. We can identify His divine fingerprints in our genetic code, called DNA, distinct to every individual created throughout human history, spanning billions and billions of people. No two people have the same genetic sequence, not even identical twins.

Not only does He design us, but He uniquely designs each of us. One person I heard described DNA like this: Divine Natural Ability, or we could say it is our Divine Natural Attributes. Divine because they are from God and natural because they are part of our nature.

LOVE - To love God is to keep His commands (1 John 5:3). Love God first, others second (Matthew 22:37–39).

People often say the greatest commandment is to love your neighbor as yourself. It's why many have an upside-down view of the gospel, where "loving" people gets distorted into affirming their life choices. When asked, Jesus said the greatest commandment was to " *'Love the Lord your God with all your heart and with all your soul and with all your mind.' This is the first and greatest commandment. And the second is like it: 'Love your neighbor as yourself'* " (Matthew 22:37–39).

We must first love God with all our heart, soul, and mind. That means obeying Him, believing in and trusting Jesus as our Lord and Savior, dedicating our lives to following His ways, and making Him known. Then, the second commandment is to love others. We will not know how to love others until we love God first.

Reversing the order of the greatest command will mean we put people above God and make God's law fit into their world rather than us fitting our lives into His.

MORALITY – It is better to obey God than ask for forgiveness (1 Samuel 15:22).

The actual Scripture says, "To obey is better than sacrifice." Out of context, this verse may sound like it's better to obey God than to sacrifice our lives, our money, our time, or something else. That's not what this verse means. Instead, it means that it is better to obey God than to ask for forgiveness through the sacrificing of animals, which was the way the Israelites atoned for their sins. God asks for our obedience. He is full of mercy and grace to forgive us our sins, but that should not be our mode of operation. Our mode of operation should be obedience first and foremost.

PURPOSE – To do the good works God prepared in advance for us to do (Ephesians 2:10) and to make disciples (Matthew 28:19–20).

Just as we are each uniquely made in the image of God, we are also uniquely purposed in His creation. There's something each of us is to do for God's Kingdom.

Raising Kingdom Builders and Disciple Makers

If we want to create our own version of Christian activists (evangelists), Kingdom builders, and disciple makers, our kids need a strong passion for knowing God and what He calls them to do.

They need salvation through Christ, a relationship with God, and the Holy Spirit to transform them into the image of Christ daily.

Part of the purpose God has called them to will include restoring culture and building it up in a way that honors God through their work. They will do that by following these commands:

- Loving God with our whole heart, soul, and mind as Jesus commanded us in the greatest commandment in Matthew 22:37–38.
- Showing the love of Christ to others as Jesus calls us to in Matthew 22:37–39.
- Making more image bearers of Christ and sharing the gospel and discipling others as we learn in Genesis 1:28 and Matthew 28:19–20.

God had a plan for us before we were born. Psalm 139:16 says, "All the days ordained for me were written in your book before one of them came to be," and Ephesians 2:10 says, "For we are God's workmanship, created in Christ Jesus to do good works, which God prepared in advance for us to do." You and I have a purpose, and our kids have a purpose to build His Kingdom here on earth, too.

Guiding our children to that purpose by recognizing their talents and considering their spiritual gifts, individual passions, and experiences, along with prayer for guidance, will help them follow God's path. Giving them space to participate in activities or volunteer in organizations that build on their passion and giftings will give them a head start on their purpose journey. Additionally, surrendering important life questions about our kids' future, like college, is essential. Sometimes, we make plans for our kids' lives without submitting them to God to see what He wants for their lives.

To see the Christian faith flourish in the next generation, we must ensure our kids are in the places God has called them to, not the places we envision them.

Our Response to Postmodern Ideas

Understanding postmodern ideology and the associated terminology is essential for parents raising Christian kids in this society. Many parents want to roll their eyes and rail against the alphabet soup. However, when we do that, we feed into the narrative our kids hear that we are ancient, don't understand modern thinking, and are not knowledgeable about how the world actually works. In other words, it diminishes our credibility with our kids.

One high school teacher told a student that her parents' Christian beliefs brainwashed them. The teacher implied it wasn't the parents' fault they didn't understand what was true and real because religion programmed them, making them incapable of seeing reality.

We are contending with this today, and we need to be wise about how we respond to our kids and, most importantly, how we equip them. We equip our kids with truth, with a biblical perspective on creation, family, evil, restoration, purpose, work, and culture. Everything we teach them about the world is directly in God's Word, which is how we form a biblical worldview and why it's so important that we read Scripture regularly.

For the rest of the book, we will explore the main critical theory disciplines in the postmodern worldview, including sexuality, gender, and race. Each of the disciplines includes its own set of vocabulary, leading causes, and solutions. However, you'll find them aligned in their activism, support of each other, and the primary ideas shared here of oppression and deconstruction.

7

Feminism's Role in Postmodernism

Feminism is a word that strikes fear in some and freedom in others. It's a word that is even divisive among Christian believers, namely women, and a movement that teen girls are jumping on the bandwagon to defend.

It may be unpopular to say this out loud or write it, but most of the social movements we are contending with and fighting against today started for important reasons. Even some that Christians should be vocal about. The issue is that when humans try to solve an area that the Bible already addresses, which is all of them, we will often be out of sync with the biblical worldview. Since Scripture defines our biblical worldview, we will ultimately be out of step with what God has designed for us.

There's no shortage of books or Bible studies today that remind us how Jesus treated women and what God thinks of them. These conversations in the church about women's worth surprised me because I thought it was obvious that women were in no way inferior to men. However, based on the popularity of this topic, it's not as obvious as I thought.

I remember having a conversation with a woman on leadership at a church as I started in women's ministry before God expanded our call to families. As I shared that God had called me to minister to women and align our thinking to Scripture, she promptly reminded me that men wrote the Bible, and therefore, it was a man's perspective, alluding that my work may be challenging. She didn't think God inspired the male writers of Scripture, but I do.

Culture has always needed God's Word to understand how to work properly. If God's Word and His standard for living were properly viewed and executed, it would work for every person in every situation, no matter their ethnicity, gender, socioeconomic status, ability, and nation of birth every single time. God does not show favoritism. His truth is available for all, and as believers, we must know and study His Word and act accordingly.

Whenever I hear a Christian woman call herself a feminist, the words of Inigo Montoya from *The Princess Bride* play in my head, "You keep using that word. I do not think it means what you think it means." I don't mean to make light of this, but words and movements matter, and how we align ourselves as Christian men and women do, too.

The feminist movement, especially for our girls, will suck them in and make a social justice warrior out of them faster than any other one. It's the first movement that half our population can immediately identify. They may not be a person of color, queer, gay, or trans, but half of our youth are female.

When Chuck Colson wrote the book *How Now Shall We Live?* over twenty years ago, he said of those leading the social justice movement, "Interestingly, six out of ten are women. They are on the cutting edge of social change, and if they are not already the dominant influence, they soon will be."[15] Judging by my social media and news feed, Colson's prediction has come true.

The majority of people fueling these social justice efforts, especially considering pro-abortion and LGBTQ+ rights, are women. In many ways, it makes sense. Women are naturally, by design, more compassionate and empathetic. They feel for the hurt, brokenness, and, at times, the injustices others have experienced. Women also have a very influential position in their homes as wives and mothers to nurture these social justice ideas.

The feminist movement has had the most impact on deconstructing our society. It's why we're covering this movement before the rest. The breakdown of ideas around sex, gender, and sexuality would not have been possible if the deconstruction of women's roles had not happened first.

So, how do we prepare our girls and boys for this conversation? How do we ensure compassion doesn't mislead our children to dismiss God's Word? We do precisely what we've been talking about ... we ground them in biblical truth and also teach them the world's perspective so they can discern what is from God and what is not.

Regarding the feminist movement, it's important to note its in flux. When the feminist movement began, college classes referred to it as women's studies. Today, you'll hear it referred to as gender studies or critical gender theory. For a long time, women's rights were the focus; now, the culture is redefining the word "woman," especially in light of the trans movement, which we will dig into in our chapter on gender and sexuality. As for the feminist movement, there's a lot to unpack here, so we should start at the beginning.

From a timeline perspective, the feminist movement officially began in 1848 at the Women's Rights Convention in Seneca Falls, New York. While it started before critical theory, it has merged into the critical theory universe and is by far the most advanced of the critical theory ideas. So much so that, to date, there are four waves of feminism. Each wave builds upon the previous one, or even evolves, based on the wave (or iteration) that came before.

The first wave of feminism, lasting from 1848 to 1920, was primarily about giving women equal rights to men, most notably the right to vote.[16]

The second wave of feminism, lasting from the 1960s to the 1990s, took off during the sexual revolution and challenged traditional women's roles. With the legalization of the pill and abortion during this time, women began focusing on their sexual freedom as well as their careers, with many of them leaving the home to pursue it.

The third wave of feminism lasted from the 1990s to the 2010s, although some may say it hasn't ended yet. This wave sought to be more inclusive of race and sexuality. Kimberle Crenshaw and her work on intersectionality influenced this new dynamic.

The fourth wave of feminism is underway and not yet defined. Its starting point coincides with the #MeToo movement. In this movement, there's a melting pot of ideas, from fighting against sexual abuse and the patriarchy (i.e., MeToo) to online activism, trans women's rights, sex and body positivity, and systemic oppression.

Some prevalent terms connected to the feminist movement are:	
Bodily autonomy	The concept that people have the right to make decisions over their own lives and bodies and should be able to do so (e.g., abortion rights)
Misogyny	Hatred, contempt, or prejudice against women
Reproductive rights	Ensuring legal rights for abortion and access to birth control
Sexism	Discrimination against women based on sex (gender)
Toxic masculinity	Traditional male roles considered harmful, such as being dominant and aggressive

These four waves highlight the evolution of the feminist movement, and these terms drive home the issues around which feminists rally. Fourth-wave feminist Nakkiah Lui sums up the movement best when she says, "I'm not a rich, white, cis, hetero-man, and I don't want to be. I don't want to have what they have. I don't want to be part of what they've created. I want to be part of a world that dismantles the values this patriarchy has defined ... I don't know what the fourth wave of feminism is. I think the strength is in our chaos, our differences unite us."[17]

That's what is most prevalent in all the critical theory solutions ... they seek to break down society and create chaos, which oddly mirrors the work of the enemy himself, specifically in the area of sex, sexuality, and gender.

Based on the critical theory framework within feminism, women are the oppressed and men (the patriarchy) are the oppressors. That's why there's typically a contempt for men within the feminist movement and a belief that dismantling the patriarchy will set women free.

One thing Summer White and Joy Temby point out on their *Sheologians* podcast is that feminism systematically unties women from their roles as wives and mothers.[18] In other words, it takes us away from God's intended design by breaking down the marriage first, the family second, our ideas about sex and sexuality next, and now the gender binary.

Especially during the second wave of feminism, we can identify some of the most far-reaching social changes that led to the breakdown of the family. For starters, the birth control pill became legal in the U.S. in 1965, making women's ability to have sex without consequences a reality and reframing the idea of family and children in the minds of women.

Next came no-fault divorce, introduced in 1969. This bill made it easy for couples to divorce without any real reason. As governor of California, Ronald Reagan was the first to legalize no-fault divorce and later admitted it was the greatest regret of his public life. From 1960 to 1980, the divorce rate more than doubled, and approximately half of the children born to married parents in the 1970s saw their parents divorce, compared to only about 11% of those born in the 1950s.[19]

Then, in 1973, the legalization of abortion further decoupled women from their role as wives and mothers. Not only that, but women were increasingly entering the workforce. With a rise in two-income households, which doubled since 1968, parents were putting their careers in the driver's seat and families in the back.

The compounded effect of these societal shifts significantly impacted marriage, family, and a child's fundamental right to grow up with their mom and dad in the home. All of these changes find their origins in the feminist movement.

Famed feminist Gloria Steinem said, "A feminist is just someone who believes in the full humanity of all people regardless of race ... of gender, of class."[20] This perspective on feminism sounds like a concept taken straight from the Bible, making it incredibly alluring to our youth. Don't we, as Christians, believe in the full humanity of all people as made in the image of God?

The quote is not the issue; the belief system behind it is. We must teach our kids to unpack words and the definitions used. For example, what does believing in "the full humanity of all people" mean? To Steinem, it means that a woman has "autonomy over her body" and can therefore end the life of her child in the womb and that we should embrace the decisions of all people even when they go against what God has called good and moral.

Teaching our kids about God's design from the youngest age (or whenever you pick up this book) is crucial. When our children see how God's design works together, they will learn to dismiss the ideas against His design as unrealistic and irrational.

So, what can we do?

To prepare our kids, we search Scripture to learn what God thinks of us. God says this about females, and this what we should teach our children:

- I made you in My image. (Genesis 1:27)
- You are my handiwork. I have preplanned work for you. (Ephesians 2:10)

- I made you perfectly. I've ordained the days of your life. (Psalm 139)
- I made you to co-rule over creation. (Genesis 1:28)
- I made you a suitable helper (completer) of your husband. (Genesis 2:18)
- I made you one flesh when you married. (Matthew 19:4–5)
- I made you to be fruitful and multiply. (Genesis 1:28)
- I transform you into the image of Christ (Galatians 5:22–25)
- I give you spiritual gifts, and you are part of the Body of Christ (1 Corinthians 12:11)
- I appointed the time you are to live and your territory. (Acts 17:26)

The kicker is that's what God says about males, too. He is speaking to us as humans made in His image. The only gender-specific verse mentioned was that a woman would be a suitable helper to her husband.

In God's view, women and men are equal in our humanness and value, but we are distinct in our roles. Women have a role as wives, complementing or completing their husbands, and as mothers in bearing children.

Gloria Steinem spoke of her draw to the women's movement because she felt boundaries in her life. She explained that those boundaries for her were bumping up against "our innate human rebellion against hierarchy."[21]

This is the plight of modern-day feminism. The very concept of rebellion against hierarchy is visible right in Scripture after the Fall, *"And you will be for your husband, and he will rule over you"* (Genesis 3:16). Thus, women's battle against hierarchy came into existence.

This age-old curse requires a biblical perspective on how to handle it. Hierarchy does not equal inferiority; it equals order. There is even hierarchy in the Trinity. God is the Father. Jesus is the Son. Jesus is always submissive to the will of the Father. That does not make Jesus less important or valuable; we would not have salvation without Him, but it does mean that hierarchy is in the very nature of God. It's evident by how He ordered the world with humans as rulers over creation and parents as overseers of their children. The concept of hierarchy is everywhere in our lives.

So, why does the hierarchy of husband over wife create such disdain? Because humans are sinful. Marriages aren't perfect; husbands fail, and so do wives. However, the Bible clearly states how humans should treat each other, specifically how men should treat their wives and women should treat their husbands. God's commands in this area are beautiful and honoring to both genders, and if we lived that way in marriage, we'd see many more marriages flourishing than floundering.

When interacting with people, the Bible tells us we should do so with gentleness, respect, graciousness, and love. After all, the second greatest commandment is to *"Love your neighbor as yourself"* (Matthew 22:39).

We can sum up the biblical worldview for relating to our spouses in marriage by Ephesians 5:21–33.

- ***"Submit to one another** out of reverence for Christ"* (Ephesians 5:21; emphasis mine). This is a command to both husbands and wives.

- *"**Wives**, submit to your husbands as to the Lord. For the husband is the head of the wife as Christ is the head of the church, his body, of which he is the Savior. Now as the church submits to Christ, so also wives should submit to their husbands"* (Ephesians 5:22–24).
- *"**Husbands**, love your wives, just as Christ loved the church and gave himself up for her to make her holy, cleansing her by the washing with water through the word, and to present her to himself as a radiant church, without stain or wrinkle or any other blemish, but holy and blameless. In this same way, husbands ought to love their wives as their own bodies. He who loves his wife loves himself. After all, no one ever hated his own body, but he feeds and cares for it, just as Christ does the church—for we are members of his body"* (Ephesians 5:25–30; emphasis mine).
- *"'**For this reason** a man will leave his father and mother and be united to his wife, and the two will become one flesh.' This is a profound mystery—but I am talking about Christ and the church. However, each one of you also must love his wife as he loves himself, and the wife must respect her husband"* (Ephesians 5:31–33).

These commands for marriage show us how well we are to treat each other. Not a husband lording power over a wife, treating her as less than, and not honoring all God has created her to be. Also, not a wife degrading, disrespecting, and emasculating her husband so that he feels less than what God created him to be. We are both image bearers of God, and both have work to do for God's Kingdom.

The union between husband and wife is powerful and can create a foundation for the family that will be unstoppable for the Kingdom of God. No wonder society and Satan want to come against it.

8

Our Culture's Sexual Obsession

As of the writing of this book, I serve on the board of a non-profit organization that will provide recovery services for male youth victims of sex trafficking. The non-profit is still in the early stages of vision planning and setup, but I've noticed that the release of a highly proclaimed movie on the topic of sex trafficking has highlighted an immense chasm between who is vocal on the subject and who is not.

In a world full of Harvey Weinsteins and a prominent social #MeToo movement that followed, progressives are eerily quiet on the topic of sex trafficking. This is out of character for a group of people who believe men in power should not abuse their power, especially with those who don't have power. That is, in essence, the heart of critical theory and precisely the dynamic that is at play in sex trafficking.

It would make sense then that the topic of sex trafficking would become the social movement of their cause, or at least one of the top three. So, why isn't it?

Unfortunately, it's an easy question to answer. If progressives went after sex trafficking, they'd have to go after the pornography industry. If they went after the pornography industry, they would have to admit that the majority of those "starring" in these films aren't actually consenting adults, which would deflate and undermine the whole consent and "ethically sourced" porn movement currently underway to break down sex and sexual and gender normativity, that is, God's design.

Pornography is one of the most powerful ways to change the sex narrative and break down the "social construct" that sex is for a man and a woman in marriage. All one has to do is get our kids watching it and addicted to it to fundamentally shift their brains from purity to immorality quicker than anything else. The rabbit hole it can pull our kids down isn't an overstatement. With algorithms that serve up increasingly perverse content and a sex drive unsatisfied with traditional sex, our kids (and adults) can find themselves in a web of perversion they never even imagined and with a sex drive that can only find satisfaction by much darker and often illegal means.

Not only are our kids given an outlet through pornography to explore all means of sexual activity, but the cultural narrative is that it is good to do so. Sex positivity is now the new buzzword; consent, rather than abstinence, is the new morality of sex, and body count is the new measurement for the number of sexual partners someone has had.

Sex positivity teaches that all consenting sexual activity is healthy and that experimentation for the sake of pleasure is good, especially outside the confines of marriage, or commitment at all, for that matter. While the pushback against a biblical perspective on sex is typically that Christian beliefs have created shame for those who want to act on their sexual desires, it's this new form of sex positivity and the consent movement that will cause the most long-term harm.

Here's why ...

The breakdown of the concept of sin.

This generation, more than any other, will have a confused understanding of what sin is and if it even matters in the Christian faith. When the lines get blurred and even crossed, and words get redefined, it's easy to get confused or even enticed into believing they don't matter anymore. If the new morality around sex is consent, then all someone has to do is say "yes," and it's okay. This is what our kids will learn is acceptable. They will not stop to ask if this will honor God, their body, their mind, or their future spouse.

This ideology seeks to destroy the concept of morality around sex. If the ideology can be successful here, then it can make us, and our kids, question whether God's rules, commands, and moral order even matter. If we stop caring about sin, then God's justice for our sin, Jesus' death on the Cross, and His Resurrection won't matter either, effectively abolishing the Christian faith.

We won't recognize that the biblical sexual ethic sets us free.

I once heard Sean McDowell say, "If we all followed the biblical sexual ethic, there would be no sexual assault, no child abuse, no pornography, no sex trafficking, no rape, no STDs, no abortion, and no divorces because of adultery. The biblical sexual ethic sets us free." He elaborates on this in his book *Chasing Love*.[22]

Let that sink in. We could eradicate most of the world's evil if we just believed and trusted God's Word and His design to be true and good. Sex without boundaries has consequences. Some of them are lifelong and irreversible.

The consent movement will be the next #MeToo movement.

Our kids will hear that as long as both people consent, then any sexual activity is okay.

But what is consent? Is it a head nod, a smile, a verbal yes, an in-depth conversation about boundaries and safe words, or a contract signed by both parties? There's a lot to consider when we talk about consent. Was the consent manipulated, coerced, strained, or non-committal?

A video from Planned Parenthood outlined this new consent movement that gained steam mainly as a response to the #MeToo movement.[23] It emphasized the need to ask for consent at each stage of the sexual process. Can I kiss you now? Can I remove your shirt? Can we try this sexual position? How about this one?

The concept of consent becomes a new form of pressure and manipulation, but now it comes with a get-out-of-jail-free card.

Is the concept of consent good? Absolutely. Will it ensure people don't feel pressured into doing something they don't want to? Sadly, I doubt it. The only thing that will change is that a girl who may have been able to say she said "no" before now must admit she said "yes." But for all the wrong reasons.

It may sound good in concept, but in reality, this movement will have many negative consequences. These young girls and boys will wind up doing many sexual deeds (way beyond the physical act of sex) that are going to leave them feeling full of shame and disgust. Self-hatred, anxiety, depression, and self-harm (cutting) are already at an all-time high among teens. Imagine how they will want to numb when they know what they have participated in goes against their own sense of morality.

This is the sad reality of this movement. It's gift wrapped as sexual freedom, but it leads to shame and sin bondage.

So, how should we teach our kids about sex?

The most important aspect of this question is that we should teach them. As parents, we should not outsource the sex conversation to the schools or even our youth pastors. Most parents would rather someone else talk to their kids about this topic than have the conversation themselves. Why? Because it's awkward; we don't want to ruin our kids' innocence; and we don't feel knowledgeable on the topic. (Does anyone else not remember that much from biology or health class?)

As conservative Christians, we are notorious for staying mum on this topic. It makes us flush and uncomfortable, but the world tells our kids EVERYTHING about sex, including sexual positions and activities we've never thought or dreamed of.

I understand the hesitancy. I was in the same boat. Then I realized that if I'm not talking to my kids first, the world will. Kids are much more apt to believe what they hear first. Most of our kids today will learn about homosexuality before they hear about God's design for sex between a husband and wife. We must hop in the driver's seat and have these crucial conversations sooner, younger, and more often than before.

There are three essentials to teach our kids about sex.

1. It's rooted in God's design and has a purpose. This mnemonic by Allie Beth Stuckey is helpful to share with our kids.[24] Sex is:

a. Rooted in Creation *for Reproduction* (addition mine) — *"So God created man in his own image ... male and female he created them. God blessed them and said to them, 'Be fruitful and increase in number; fill the earth and subdue it' "* (Genesis 1:27–28).

b. Reiterated in Scripture — Scripture positively defines marriage as between one man and one woman (Genesis 2:24).

c. Repeated by Jesus Himself — *"Haven't you read ... at the beginning the Creator 'made them male and female,' and said, 'For this reason a man will leave his father and mother and be united to his wife, and the two will become one flesh'? So they are no longer two, but one. Therefore what God has joined together, let man not separate"* (Matthew 19:4–5).

d. Representative of Christ and the Church — Earthly picture of the eternal union between Christ as the groom and the Church as the bride. It has earthly and eternal significance (Ephesians 5:22–33).

e. Reflective of the Gospel — The gospel starts with the marriage of Adam and Eve in the Garden and ends with the marriage of Christ and the Church.

2. We discover God's goodness in His boundaries.

This is a foundational belief of the Christian faith. We understand that God is good and holy, and because He is good and holy, He has set up rules for us that are good and holy. Not to punish or keep us captive but because we experience harm when we don't do things God's way. There are unwanted consequences that we could have to live with forever, like sexually transmitted diseases, intrusive and reoccurring thoughts, or shame and disgust. God knew what He was doing when He created boundaries for us, and it wasn't to keep us from all the fun but to protect us from all the heartache. God created sex, after all, and what He created is good in the proper context of marriage.

In the act of sex between a husband and a wife, God is also making His Word about the two becoming one flesh a reality. As Hillary Ferrer and Amy Davison point out in *Mama Bear Apologetics Guide to Sexuality*, during sexual activity, the bonding chemicals oxytocin and vasopressin release, further connecting the two (husband and wife) as one.[25] It's not just a spiritual metaphor, it's a physical occurrence.

3. There's grace and forgiveness when we mess up.

We have all needed God's grace and forgiveness. Jesus' forgiveness is what brings so many of us sinners to our knees in gratitude and surrender. It's essential to ensure our kids know that nothing too big or too small can separate them from the love of Christ. It's tempting as parents not to lead with God's grace because we fear our kids may latch on to it and make poor decisions. However, grace is essential to the gospel, so we must ensure they know this. Our kids won't truly understand the gospel without an environment of grace in our homes.

It's also important for us as parents to consider how we will respond if our child shares with us; for example, he or she is watching porn. Will we shame our kids and make them feel disgusted with themselves (like they probably already feel), or will we talk to them about God's love, forgiveness, and restoration? What if our daughter comes home with a positive pregnancy test? Or tells us she's gay?

How we respond in these raw and vulnerable moments will impact our relationship with our children and their trust in us. Will we be someone they can count on and confide in – not to tell them what they did is okay, but to help them through it? Consider practicing your response to these challenging scenarios ahead of time to take the sting out of it. Hopefully, you'll never have to find out how you'd respond, but too many Christian parents have heard these words from their kids and wished they had a do-over.

Most notably, on the topic of sex, we need to be the authority in our kids' lives. Authority comprises three things: position, knowledge, and relationship. We already have a position of authority in our kids' lives because God made us the parents, but do we have the necessary knowledge and a relationship with our kids that invites an open dialogue?

Now, a few more words to the wise about the sex talk ...

- As early as age three, you can start talking about the God-designed differences between males and females that we cover in the next chapter. This will reiterate to your kids that God has order in the way He designed us and will help ensure that when our kids hear of gender fluidity and sexuality, they don't accept it as fact but see it as fiction.
- Always use proper names for body parts and functions – vagina and penis, for example. This will remind your kids that you are credible and not using cartoon language for actual parts. You can also introduce the word "sex" and let your child know it's between husband and wife before you ever need to explain the mechanics of it. This is helpful so that it's not a foreign concept by the time you get to the detailed conversation.
- By age 10, before 5th grade, your kids should understand how sex works. You can start this conversation sooner, but if you wait any longer, they will hear about it from friends,

impacting your ability to be the authority. Here's the format I followed, and you can too. It emphasizes the binary of male and female, when life is created (pro-life), how life is created, and the importance of sex within marriage.

Start with Gender

Our sex chromosomes determine gender.

Women have XX chromosomes, and men have XY chromosomes.

Only a biological male and biological female can create a baby.

Reminder of God's Design for Sex

(See Allie Beth Stuckey's mnemonic above)

Explain the Act of Sex

If helpful, show an image of the male and female reproductive systems.

Explain the act of sex/intercourse.

Explain the baby-making process.

Conception begins when the sperm fertilizes the egg.

The father's sex chromosomes determine gender — he either gives the baby an X or Y chromosome.

Once a baby is made, the child has unique DNA and is a life.

Prepare Yourself with an Educational Video.

Search YouTube™, and you'll find one.

- For kids 11+, use the proper terms for body functions, sexual activity, and sexual pleasure. Yes, *those* words!

Also, if your child is in middle school and you have yet to have this conversation with them, set a date in the next month and make this a priority. You may need to assert yourself as the authority because they have already heard so much and know much more than you think. It may be appropriate to approach it by saying, "Hey, we (Mom and Dad) want to apologize because we thought we had more time, but we realize we should have been talking to you much sooner on this topic."

As Christian parents, we have to ensure that we have fully prepared our kids on this topic. We also must ensure we haven't kept them in the dark on essential conversations because we assume they will never do it. We also don't want to assume our kids will. To educate your kids, you can say something like, "If your friends ever start to have sex or participate in sexual activity, then they need to know this." It's a way of educating your child without assuming he or she will do it. These are also the topics your school's sex talk will cover. For specifics, you should always be able to get an outline from the school. That way, if you opt out of the school sex talk, like us, you have talking points to cover with your kids as you see fit.

- **Agreement** – Ensure sexual activity is consensual and never forced. No means no.
- **Protection** – Condoms and birth control can prevent pregnancies and STDs. You can reiterate these are not foolproof options. Please note that I am not advocating for contraceptive promotion to our children, rather simply saying our children need to be informed on this topic.
- **Consequences** – There are consequences to sex, like sexually transmitted diseases, pregnancy, rumors, and negative

impact on reputation, and it's easier to have sex again once you've gone down that path.

Okay, that sums up the sex talk portion of our regularly scheduled programming. If this felt stressful, I get it. Being the authority on the topic of sex means having hard conversations and stepping up to the plate to have them. Keeping these discussions matter of fact and light in tone with your kids will ensure the dialogue is easy and conversational rather than difficult and uncomfortable.

The Explosive Growth of LGBTQ+ Ideology

According to the CDC, 1 out of 4 teens now identify as LGBTQ+. This is up from 1 in 10 just six years earlier. The acceleration of the ideology is mind-blowing but not surprising, considering the breakdown of the family, sex, sexuality, and gender that we've watched unfold.

When we break down any belief system, all of them are up for grabs. Now that the culture has successfully broken down the norm for sexual intercourse and blamed society for forcing its belief system on others, conversations around gender and homosexuality become normal.

Not only is the conversation normalized, but it is now attached to our fundamental identity. Expressing preferred pronouns is just as prevalent for our kids as saying, "I have brown hair and blue eyes." There's also a social stigma with not going along with the pronoun phenomenon. Just ask any kid who has refused to share their pronouns on the first day of high school or doesn't add she/her, he/him, or they/them in their social media profile.

It's also important to note that there's a fundamental shift in the way society is talking about gender and sexuality. The days when gender and biological sex were the same thing are long gone. In her book *Love Thy Body*, Christian author Nancy Pearcey explains the separation between body and mind that is promoted nowadays, as if they're not interconnected and part of one whole. This belief system disassociates someone's biological sex (body) from their gender identity (mind).[26]

Popular critical queer theorist Judith Butler expresses the idea like this, "Gender is not something that one is, it is something that one does, an act ... a 'doing' rather than a 'being.'"[27] She asserts that gender is more about our actions and the gender we assign to those actions as a society rather than gender being a distinction innate to us.

This belief system, called critical queer theory, is the application of the critical theory framework to gender and sexual identity. From a critical queer theory perspective, the binary of male and female is a social construct, as is sex between a man and a woman — meaning it's just something society decides and not something that's true. Because of this, one must deconstruct society's beliefs about gender and sexuality and then reconstruct and re-envision them. In the latest iteration of this belief system, gender and sexuality are fluid and can therefore change. Gender and sexuality are also on a spectrum, so there's an associated range from feeling male to female, for example.

Along with these ideas, we now have a new language associated with the movement. Words like trans, pan, nonbinary, and cisgender express various gender and sexual identities. There's also new language to depict the culture of the movement, like glitter families, deadnames, misgendering, coming-out parties, and pronouns, including the newly created gender-neutral pronouns zie and hir. Familiar words and phrases from the postmodern worldview, like allies, intersectionality, and social construct, are also present in this ideology.

Queer is also no longer a derogatory word. It identifies anyone who doesn't conform to traditional beliefs about gender and sexuality.

Abigail Shrier, author of *Irreversible Damage*, who writes about the sudden contagion since 2012 of girls who want to become boys, says, "Many of the adolescent girls who adopt a transgender identity have never had a single sexual or romantic experience. They have never been kissed by a boy or girl. What they lack in life experience, they make up for with a sex-studded vocabulary and avant-garde gender theory."[28]

The conversation has moved beyond people who genuinely experience gender dysphoria or same-sex attraction to an enticement into experimentation and exploration. The ideology is particularly attractive to children and teens who are dealing with anxiety and depression and who have unrestricted access to social media. The combination makes them vulnerable to believing the messages they hear and accepting that this belief system will heal their hurts.

There is now even a process, or we can liken it to a formula, to determine someone's gender identity. Trans Student Educational

Resources (TSER) introduced the Gender Unicorn in 2015, a cartoon unicorn graphic that explains the five components of gender identity so a child can identify where he or she falls on the spectrum of each of the five points.[29] Introduced in a school district in North Carolina, this resource created an outcry in 2017 when presented to kids as young as kindergarten. While there's not a listing of all the states that use this resource, for school districts that give their teachers discretion on what resources to introduce to their students, the Gender Unicorn is inevitably used by some who wish to promote this ideology.

As parents, we must understand the five points of gender identity and how the culture, and the Gender Unicorn, breaks it down.

Gender Identity	One's internal sense of being male, female, neither of these, both, or another gender(s)
Gender Expression	Representing one's gender identity through clothing, hairstyle, voice, body shape, etc.
Sex Assigned at Birth (Biological Sex)	The assignment of people as male, female, or intersex based on a combination of anatomy, hormones, and chromosomes; biological sex
Physically Attracted To	Sexual orientation
Emotionally Attracted To	Romantic/emotional orientation

These five components help a child determine where they fall on the LGBTQ+ spectrum. The Gender Unicorn is distinctively kid-like to appeal to young ones. It is also built like a quiz so you can figure out your gender and sexual identity as you compare the findings to the definitions of LGBTQ+ identities. For example, if a teen has a gender identity and gender expression of a girl but has a sex assigned at birth that's male, then the boy would identify as a trans woman. Alternatively, if a teen indicates that they experience physical and emotional attraction to men, women, and other genders, then that teen is pansexual, regardless of their gender identity. Ultimately, the selections from the Gender Unicorn graphic correlate to a gender or sexual identity designation from the LGBTQ+ lexicon. There is a method to the madness.

One thing we, as parents, neglect to recognize is that critical theory, including critical queer theory, is an ideology founded in academia. Intellectuals, professors, and philosophers are all part of the conversation and the advancement of the belief system. Because of this, they ground their language and ideas in intelligent technical speak that has an air of advancement about them. This means they seem progressive and intellectual, making them appealing and credible to our youth and even some adults.

For this reason, when we roll our eyes and make fun of the ideology, we can look like the dumb ones to our kids. Rather than demean the ideology, we must prepare to have intellectual conversations with our kids and talk through the ideas of the postmodern worldview versus what the Bible (and biology) teaches us about the world and our identity.

One of the biggest criticisms of critical theory is that with the elevation of one minority group above the other, the elevated one becomes the oppressor group. In other words, as one group grows in power, another group gets pushed down to the oppressed (powerless) category, making this an ideology that doesn't solve power dynamics; it just makes it a cyclical process that keeps reoccurring. This is especially evident in the current women's and trans rights movements. Today's belief system suggests that a man who identifies as a woman (a trans woman) is an actual woman and can access the same rights as a woman, including playing in women's sports, for example. In this instance, trans women (biological men) are now oppressing biological women.

In a similar situation, I learned of an organization helping girls in lower-income countries access education they would not usually have access to. As I did some research on this organization, I found this definition of "girls" as part of their foundational statement, "The term girls is inclusive of all individuals who identify with the experiences of girls, including gender-nonconforming, genderfluid, transfeminine experiences, up to the age of 22." This is another example where trans women are oppressing biological females.

TERFs are feminists who support abortion and LGBTQ+ rights but oppose having trans women (biological men) take rights and experiences away from biological women. This derogatory term stands for Trans Exclusionary Radical Feminists. These are feminists who may respect and fight for trans rights but ultimately don't believe trans women are actual women, as the ideology insists. *Harry Potter* author J.K. Rowling, accused of being a TERF, emphatically and unashamedly states that gender (aka sex) is real. Specifically, she tweeted, "If biological sex isn't real, there's no same-sex attraction. If biological sex isn't real, the lived reality of women globally is erased." So, even within the ideology, there's a tension brewing.

I recently brought two news articles to our student worldview and apologetics class. One article was about a young white girl who identified as Asian, a term called transracialism. The other article was about a woman who married an AI (artificial intelligence).

Each article highlighted the future ideas these students will be contending with as they continue to become mainstream, which they will. As we start to break down that which is obvious, scientifically proven, and biblically promoted (sex, gender, marriage, life, ethnicity), we make room for a whole new realm of thought that will continue to degrade what God created.

The assault on sex, gender, marriage, life, and ethnicity is all a way of tearing us away from what God called good and what He ordered. Postmodernism and critical theory aren't ultimately an assault on power dynamics; they're an assault on Christianity.

Even prior to the acceleration of the trans movement, it's safe to say that Christians have not always been compassionate to those struggling with same-sex attraction. Decades ago, it was not uncommon to hear of Christian families who would disown their child who struggled with it. We are now experiencing the culture's reaction to a harsh response that some people who genuinely struggled may have received.

In this way, postmodern activists view the Church and Christians as the oppressors (those with power) and those in the LGBTQ+ community as the oppressed (those without power). The Church is the enemy, and those who identify as LGBTQ+ are the victims. This idea alone has caused much contempt for the Church and a backlash against biblically based beliefs because it is the Bible, not man, who gives us the concept of the binary of male and female, and sex between husband and wife.

So, what are we to do with all this coming at our kids?

Root them in God's design, teach them to find their identity in Christ, and respond compassionately to those struggling with their identity. For starters:

Teach Your Kids the Five Differences of Male and Female

Just as the Gender Unicorn offers five components of gender identity, we also have five divinely designed differences between male and female that we can see in Scripture and science. Men and women are different spiritually, mentally, emotionally, physically, and sexually. Educating our kids on the differences between male and female, starting as early as we can, will form their understanding of the binary of male and female and that we are fundamentally different based on how God designed us.

1. **Spiritually** – Both men and women are made in the image of God, meaning we have equal value in the eyes of God, yet He designed us differently to complement each other. Biblical womanhood reinforces that God designed women with compassion, wisdom, conscientiousness, industriousness, and in service to others. Biblical manhood includes protection, provision, sacrificial love, and family leadership. In marriage, the husband is the spiritual leader of the home, and the wife is the perfect gap filler, as two puzzle pieces come together to form one flesh.
2. **Mentally** – Based on brain development, girls mature two to three years faster than boys. Men have more grey matter while women have more white matter, which is why women are better at multitasking and men are better at staying on task.

   Additionally, women use both sides of the brain for verbal processing, making them more talkative, while men primarily use the left side, making them more focused. Brain connections move front to back for men versus side to side for women, making men better problem solvers. One part of the brain linked with mathematical problem solving, estimating time, and judging speed is larger in men (the inferior parietal lobule) than in women.[30]

3. **Emotional** – Women's brains have greater blood flow to specific regions, which makes women more empathetic and intuitive but also more prone to anxiety and depression. Female brains also show higher activity levels in the limbic system, critical for bonding, nesting, and emotions, explaining why women are generally the primary caretakers of children.[31]
4. **Physically** – Once puberty hits for males, they grow taller, weightier, and have more upper body strength. Testosterone is higher in men, which is essential for sperm production. It helps men build more muscle mass and burn fat more effectively. Estrogen is higher in women, which is essential for breast development and the menstrual cycle.
5. **Sexually** – Women have XX sex chromosomes, while men have XY sex chromosomes. The Y chromosome for men is responsible for the creation of male genitalia. Most importantly, males and females have different reproductive systems (testicles and sperm for men; ovaries, eggs, and a uterus for women) essential for the production of life. Without this difference, humankind would cease to exist. The woman's body is created to carry life and sustain it after birth through milk production.

God created men and women differently by design. No number of surgeries, hormone replacement therapies, or medications can effectively or sufficiently change what God has made in the binary of male and female to complete each other and produce children.

It's beautiful to see that as we consider our differences mentally, emotionally, physically, and sexually, it maps directly to how God created us spiritually. Our God is the God of order and design. What God has made is good and necessary to fulfill His purpose for us.

Understand the Ideology and the Terminology

As shared, it's critical that we have a healthy understanding of the belief system our kids will encounter and that we do not mock it, but rather provide evidence as to why it's a false ideology. Knowing not only the five points of gender identity, but also the terminology will help ensure that we are credible in our kids' eyes. One mom shared that after attending one of our classes, she began having more conversations with her child on the topic of gender and sexual identity. The child was even confident confiding in the mom because of her knowledge. The mom was able to walk through a difficult season with her child as a result. What a blessing. Knowledge equates to authority and credibility.

With that in mind, some popular terms to know are:	
Cisgender	Someone whose gender identity matches their biological sex; e.g., a person who identifies as a man and is biologically a man.
Coming-out parties	An event celebrating a person's LGBTQ+ identity.
Deadnaming	Using someone's birth name and not their new preferred name.
Furries	People interested in anthropomorphized animals and dressing up like them.

Gender dysphoria	A feeling of distress that results when someone believes their gender identity doesn't match his or her biological sex.
Gender fluid	A person who does not confine themselves to one gender or another.
LGBTQQIA	An extension to LGBTQ+ that includes lesbian, gay, bi (bisexual), trans, queer, questioning, intersex, asexual/agender.
Misgendering	Not using someone's preferred pronouns.
Nonbinary	Someone who does not conform to the binary of male or female.
Pan (pansexual)	Someone who is attracted to an individual regardless of gender, also considered gender-blind.
Queer	Someone who does not conform to traditional beliefs about gender and sexual identity.
Trans	A person whose gender identity does not match their biological sex; e.g., a person who identifies as a man but is biologically a woman (a trans man).

Reiterate Our Identity in Christ

See Chapter 5 on the biblical worldview, and explain what it means to be made in the image of God with your child. As believers, our identity is in God, not man's definitions.

Remind Our Kids that Jesus Did Speak on These Topics.

It's a popular narrative in today's culture to suggest that Jesus did not speak on the topic of sex, marriage, or gender. However, based on several key passages, Jesus was clear on these matters.

- Jesus talked about sex:

  "What comes out of a person is what defiles them. For it is from within, out of a person's heart, that evil thoughts come — ***sexual immorality****, theft, murder,* ***adultery****, greed, malice, deceit, lewdness, envy, slander, arrogance and folly. All these evils come from inside and defile a person"* (Mark 7:20–23; emphasis mine).

- Jesus talked about marriage between a man and woman:

  " 'For this reason a ***man*** *shall leave his father and mother and be joined to his* ***wife****, and the two shall become one flesh'; so then they are no longer two, but one flesh. Therefore what God has joined together, let not man separate"* (Mark 10:7–9; emphasis mine).

- Jesus talked about the binary of male and female:

  "But from the beginning of the creation, God 'made them ***male*** *and* ***female****' "* (Mark 10:6; emphasis mine).

Show Compassion and Discuss with Your Kids Why Someone May Identify as Gay or Trans.

There are many reasons why someone may believe they are gay, including, but not limited to:	
Natural inclination	Some may experience a natural inclination toward same-sex attraction. While this, at times, could be the sole reason, there are often other reasons why someone may have this attraction.
Suffered from abuse	It's not uncommon, for example, for females who have suffered from sexual, physical, or emotional abuse at the hands of a male to have a deep-seated discomfort or fear of men and seek female companionship as a result. It's also not uncommon for males abused by males to form a belief that because their bodies physically responded to the sexual abuse, they are gay (same for females abused by females).
Suffered from an absentee parent	It's also not uncommon for females who have had an absentee father and have suffered from hurt and abandonment as a result to seek relationships with other females, and vice versa for males.

Pornography	When someone watches pornography, they become physically aroused and even mentally and emotionally bonded with what they're viewing. It's the express purpose of pornography to create this arousal and connection. If someone views same-sex pornography, they can come to believe their arousal means they are gay.
Experimentation	Some people decide to experiment sexually. It's not an "orientation" but rather a desire to try new things that create sexual pleasure.
Rejection	When rejected by someone of the opposite sex but accepted by someone of the same sex, a person can easily fall into the lifestyle as a means to feel desired and accepted.
Desire to fit in	It's common for children to want to fit in with their peer groups. Because of this, they may place an identity on themselves to fit in with their friend group.

Many decisions to adopt an LGBTQ+ identity come from pain and a numbing from abandonment, rejection, a desire for acceptance, and many other reasons. We need to recognize that many times, people are hurting. Showing Christ's love can go a long way to heal the brokenness and point people to the only One who can genuinely heal: Jesus.

For all these reasons, a person may identify as trans as well.

Additionally, with transgenderism, there is a masking element to the belief. Think of an actor who gets on stage and inhabits a new persona. Rather than being their authentic selves, like society would have us believe transgender people are being, there is often something underneath the surface that makes this child want to put on the mask and disappear into a whole new reality. They want to forget who they are and escape into something new.

A video I recently watched from Axis on the furry phenomenon had a similar message. They noted that children could be very introverted and shy, but then suddenly became silly, fun, and outgoing when wearing their furry costumes. It allowed the child to become someone (or, in this case, something) else.[32]

So, how may the "mask" be helping a trans-identifying youth?

- **Protection** – As with being gay, it's not uncommon for people who identify as trans to have suffered abuse at some point in their lives. It could be physical abuse or sexual abuse, mental or emotional. As an example, if it was sexual abuse, a young girl may think it will be safer for her to be a male (or vice versa for boys) so that she won't endure the abuse any longer.
- **Hiding out** – If a child doesn't like their body or who they are and feels shame because of it, the child may decide it is better to resurrect a new image than be vulnerable living as who they are and exposed to self-criticism or bullying.
- **Comfort** – Like cutting, drinking, or drugs, the child may feel comfort in this new persona that essentially soothes and numbs them from either the real or perceived harsh or difficult realities of their life. The new identity becomes like a security blanket.

- **Same-sex attraction** – Some of our Christian youth who are turning to trans ideology may be doing so because they experience same-sex attraction, which they know the Bible speaks against. Rather than live in sin, they rationalize it would be better to be the opposite gender so they are no longer technically same-sex attracted. Someone may reason that being a trans woman who likes a male is better than a boy who likes a boy, for example.

When you see or meet a youth who identifies as LGBTQ+, pray for them and teach your kids to do the same. Pray that God would heal their hearts, change their minds, and point their gaze on Him. Pray also that God would bring people into their lives who will love them and speak biblical truth with compassion. Also, pray for their parents, who are undoubtedly struggling and deeply impacted by their child's decisions. Understand that not all kids who identify as LGBTQ+ are trying to be edgy or rebellious. Many are genuinely hurting and need Jesus to heal them.

God has called us to love others and to be a city on a hill. How we treat people through this challenging time matters in the Kingdom of God and to our witness in their lives. As parents, our kids may come home one day telling us of a friend who is now LGBTQ+, or they may struggle with it themselves. If we have been condescending and hateful to those in this lifestyle, we may very well become the enemy in our kids' eyes, or at least someone they distrust. We will then have missed our opportunity to minister and love well and to teach them to do the same.

As a word of encouragement to any parents whose child struggles with any aspect of LGBTQ+ ideology, please know there is hope and you're not alone. We are so blessed to have Christians who have come out of the LGBTQ+ lifestyle, live God-honoring lives, and are willing to share their experiences. The process is not always easy or quick, but our God is in the restoration business. Authors like Christopher Yuan, with his book *Holy Sexuality and the Gospel*, and Jackie Hill-Perry, with her book *Gay Girl, Good God*, are excellent resources. Additionally, *Irreversible Damage* by Abigail Shrier is a helpful look at the trans movement and its impact on girls.

There are organizations like ours, Genuine Family Ministries, and my friend Mary Comm's ministry, Uncommon Love (who has a book by the same name), actively ministering to parents of LGBTQ+-identifying children. As I write this, our non-profit is also determining how to build a nationwide network to mentor trans-identifying teens with biblical discipleship. Moreover, we are not the only ones stepping into this space to minister with biblical truth and grace. Please remember that you do have help, resources, and people who will stand with you as you walk this difficult journey. God has not forgotten you or your child.

I once heard it said that "the church will be responsible for picking up the pieces of the sexual revolution," and that's what we and many others aim to do with biblical truth and love, never forsaking one for the other, just as Jesus did.

10

The Problem of Justice

Ibram X. Kendi shares a story in his book *How to Be an Antiracist* that strikes at the core of the problems in our culture's current conversation around justice. He talks about the day the jury acquitted O.J. Simpson and how his (Kendi's) dad and all their friends celebrated the not-guilty verdict. They rejoiced in watching Simpson, a black man, go free.[33]

We could reasonably understand if Kendi, his father, and their friends praised the verdict because they believed O.J. to be genuinely innocent and wrongly accused. It would be a day to triumph and thank God for a victory. However, that's not why they cheered.

They celebrated because this black man, who they also assumed was guilty, was found innocent. These men reasoned that since the justice system found many white men innocent of crimes they committed, it was actually justice for O.J. that injustice was served.

Kendi expressly states this concept in his book – injustice is okay when that injustice makes up for past or present injustices. So, what do we do with a postmodern worldview focused on injustice that also promotes injustice?

The biggest challenge Christians, or more specifically, our kids, have today in the culture is the topic of justice. Why? Because our Scripture hinges on it. The death, burial, and Resurrection of Jesus is God's justice on display. It was His justice in action. Definitions of justice can get quickly intertwined if we are unclear about what the definitions mean.

In one situation, a teacher did an entire talk on social justice (critical theory style) and bathed it in verses about justice from the Bible. When approached about the obvious social justice themes shared in the teaching, like white privilege and Jesus speaking truth to power, the administration shut down the conversation. After all, the teacher used a ton of Bible verses to make a point, so it must be correct, right?

Sadly, that's what we are dealing with when discussing justice. Because what is biblical justice, really? How do we define it as Christians, and how does it relate to caring for widows and orphans versus individuals or people groups mistreated or hated because of the color of their skin or the nation of their ancestry?

And what about the topic of representation? Can't we all agree that for minorities, what a beautiful thing it must be to see themselves on the movie screen or portrayed in a book? Isn't it good for all of us to see the diversity God created in our lives? When does representation then become less about physical traits, as image bearers of God, and more about sexual and gender identity embraced by individuals?

This is a complicated topic when talking with teens because they, too, see representation as good. I do as well, except when it comes to the LGBTQ+ lifestyle or when the solutions push a new form of injustice. In fact, according to research, 79% of people ages 18–24 believe that white people are oppressors and non-white people are the oppressed, highlighting the advancement of this ideology among the younger generation.[34]

If you've ever watched a recreated video of Drs. Kenneth and Mamie Clark's doll test, where they ask black children to pick between a black and white doll and decide which one was pretty, ugly, good, or bad, then undoubtedly you were heartbroken just like me.[35] Most children picked the white doll as both pretty and good, subsequently identifying the black doll as ugly and bad. The doctors then asked black children which doll most resembles themselves, and they select the black doll. The sadness in their eyes as they realize they relate to the "ugly, bad doll" is enough to make you cry and rethink the effects skin tone has in our culture.

So, what should we do when we know the God of all creation created all of us in His image, and that the versatility He created through skin tone, eye color, hair texture, height differences, and beyond, is as majestic as how He created the variety of flowers in the fields? Or when we know there's real brokenness and hurt that people of color have experienced merely for the melanin in their skin?

The problem of justice in our society ultimately comes down to the solution. What do we define as injustice, and how do we solve the problem? Will we use the Bible as our guide or man-made solutions?

As we dive into the topic, we must understand the postmodern solution based on critical race theory and the biblical perspective of justice. This will help us and our kids discern what truth to follow and what lies to ignore.

I once heard Os Guinness outline biblical justice like this:

Firstly: Biblical justice calls for repentance, turning from one's sins or wrongdoings.

Secondly: Biblical justice calls for confession by taking personal responsibility and accountability.

Thirdly: Biblical justice calls for forgiveness, where the past does not define us and there's hope for the future.

Lastly: Biblical justice calls for reconciliation to the Lord, human to human, and within families and communities.[36]

It sounds a lot like our gospel. Moreover, it sounds like the framework for which we built our modern-day justice system. That's because it is.

This is the meaning of a biblical worldview, to understand God's idea of justice through Scripture and to apply it to our lives, families, communities, and even our judicial system. If there was no God and the world exploded into place by accident, then there would be no concept of justice and injustice, good and evil, or right and wrong. Since God does exist and sets a moral infrastructure for us to live by, we can judge between what is good and evil. We can also understand how to handle unjust situations and ensure justice happens.

So, then, what is a biblical definition of justice? Biblical justice makes things right according to God's standard of righteousness (goodness, holiness, and morality). In the sense of the gospel, God required that sinful people be righteous before Him to reunite with Him, which could only happen by the shedding of Jesus' blood to atone for the sins of all who believe.

How, then, do we apply that idea of justice to everyday situations, or in the case of this topic, racism? Since we are all made in the image of God, then it is unjust to treat people also made in the image of God as inferior in any way.

I remember when George Floyd died. I'm sure most of us do because it set off a firestorm in this nation amid the global pandemic of 2020. It was these two events together that created irreparable harm in this nation. After it, we saw more significant divisions created than ever before and a rampant acceleration of progressive, anti-biblical ideology like never before.

When George Floyd's death, captured on video, circulated online, there was an immediate outcry. Black squares flooded social media, including by many Christians, as a sign of solidarity with him and the plight of the Black Lives Matter movement. My heart was heavy, and I attempted multiple times to write my black square post to demonstrate my sadness for what felt like a very senseless loss of life. I remember telling my husband that I struggled to write the post because I didn't ultimately know what I was trying to say. Was I saying the policeman was wrong, or that police officers everywhere were wrong, or that George Floyd was innocent, or that I was in alignment with the Black Lives Matter movement? Ultimately, I was in no place to have an opinion on any of that, with so much still unknown at the time of the event. My husband wisely said, "Then maybe you shouldn't post anything about it at all." So, I didn't.

Months later, as I began to understand the ideology of critical race theory, I was very thankful I didn't comply with a knee-jerk reaction to align to a movement that ultimately is not about God's justice but about man's.

What I do most vividly remember, though, from George Floyd's heartbreaking death was asking God to search me and know me and see if there is any offensive way in me. The situation made me question whether any prejudice existed in my heart. If it did, I asked God to rid me of it and to see all people, regardless of age, skin color, or socioeconomic status, as made in the image of God.

There's merit to race conversations in America, to discussing people's difficult and painful experiences, to understanding where and how we can ensure a more just society in areas like education, housing, and jobs, to asking God to search us and know us and see if there is any offensive way in us. There's merit to many of the race conversations in America, but we must first answer those questions about how we are defining injustice and the solution. Here, we will be able to clearly delineate between what is biblical and what is not.

Two of the most popular books that emerged in many Christian book circles in the aftermath of George Floyd included *How to Be an Antiracist* by Ibram X. Kendi and *White Fragility* by Robin DiAngelo. Christians sought answers to racial reconciliation and unity, and these books were the available options. Sadly, many Christians who formed community healing groups around these books likely had no idea where the ideas stemmed from or who they were taking notes from. Kendi and DiAngelo are neither self-professing Christians nor profess to be students of God's Word. Why is this important? Because they aren't providing a perspective on how to solve injustice from a biblical worldview. Instead, they solve it from a postmodern worldview steeped in critical theory.

As shared in a previous chapter, critical theory is the idea that the only evil in society is oppression, or racism in this case, and that we redeem society by making right the wrongs against the oppressed by shifting the power dynamic in society. Terms like social constructs, deconstruction, social justice warriors, intersectionality, lived experiences, allyship, and DEI (diversity, equity, and inclusion) are standard across all oppressed groups. While these words span race, gender, sexuality, and any other minority group, there are ideas more specific to critical race theory, including white privilege, antiracism, and systemic racism, and there are causes more central to critical race theory activists like defunding the police, prison reform, and reparations.

Critical race theory (CRT) applies critical theory ideas to race/ethnicity/skin tone. Today, the definition of racism is changing. No longer is it about discrimination or unequal opportunities, it's about equity. Equity is equal outcomes produced by rearranging scoreboards in favor of the oppressed in order to redeem the wrongs of the past.

This new postmodern definition suggests that everyone is racist, that it may not even be our fault, but white people specifically need to own it to fix it, which is the basic concept of white privilege. We must be antiracist, not simply "not a racist," which means we must actively promote antiracist ideas and push for change, not just talk about it. Moreover, any injustice to someone of color is racism, whether intentional or not, or based on discrimination or not. If you are a person of color, you are automatically the victim of racism. The concept of assimilation, meaning the blending of cultures that most of us grew up with, is also now racist.

Additionally, critical race theory teaches that racism is embedded in our systems (systemic racism), or the infrastructures in our society, like the justice system, police forces, housing industry, and even in our churches. Therefore, we need to deconstruct, or tear down, these systems in order to rebuild them in a way that takes into consideration our new definition of racism and our concept of equity. As Kendi says, "If discrimination is creating equity, then it's antiracist. If discrimination is creating inequity, then it's racist."[37]

Kendi also explicitly states that to be an antiracist, one must also be for all the lived experiences of black people, including their gender and sexual identities. If you do not support them and their identities, then you are not an antiracist. He conflates race, gender, and sexual identity, making them a package deal.

These ideas have also made their way into the Church through progressive "Christianity," with ideas that Jesus just came to speak truth to power, bring down the patriarchy, and set the captives free. Essentially, it reimagines what Jesus came to do. Rather than forgiving us our sins, Jesus came to shift the power dynamic, making Him the ultimate social justice warrior.

There are several reasons why social justice doesn't align with biblical justice outlined in Scripture. For starters, and most importantly, it relies solely on a works-based, man-made redemption, removing Jesus from the process. It suggests that man can redeem society through our work to deconstruct society and create equity. In this way, true restoration and justice can never occur because man's work is never enough, and no amount of work will ever completely satisfy past injustices. It counters our belief in Jesus and the finality of the atoning work on the Cross that covers past, present, and future sins of all who repent, believe, and follow Him.

Additionally, as equity shifts the power dynamic from oppressed to oppressor, a new class of oppressed forms (i.e., reversed racism) and elevates one race or "lived experience" over another. It also suggests that the only human sin is racism or oppression, leaving out all the other sins God defines, such as murder, lying, and sexual immorality. Ultimately, it sets up the belief that there is no moral standard by which all should live other than to overturn power structures.

These reasons express why social and biblical justice are at odds and cannot live together. However, we know that racism does occur and that it is sinful when it does. We also know that hurt exists from people wrongly treated and that ignoring the pain or injustices that have occurred does not help people heal, reconcile where needed, or ensure justice. So, what can we do?

We can listen, show compassion, ask questions of those hurting, and teach our kids to do the same. We can understand the biblical idea of justice and seek out resources based on a biblical worldview to equip us for conversations and to make changes in society where needed. There's no doubt that God is calling some of His people, including our kids, into the biblical justice space, like He has with the founders of the Center for Biblical Unity.

I remember hearing Monique Duson from the Center for Biblical Unity at a worldview conference I attended. It was 2021, and she started her talk by saying, "Hi, my brothers and sisters," to a room full of white people. The crowd roared and clapped, thankful to hear a black woman expressing her love for and unity with everyone in the room.

Later, I learned about the work of not only Monique but also Krista Bontrager. I enjoyed listening to their talks on culture's view of racial reconciliation and the Church's role in biblical unity conversations, and learning about their workshops and resources on the topic. They are a blessing to this conversation on how the Church and Christians should approach this sensitive and critical topic from a biblical worldview.

At that conference, Monique, a former social justice warrior turned biblical worldview warrior, shared a few concepts regarding how Christians should think about race. She reminded us that we are all made in the image of God; that sin ruins everything, making us prone to wrongdoing; that God does not show favoritism; and that, as Christians, we are all a family and heirs to the Kingdom of God.

She said, "Being antiracist will never rid us of racism," because of the inherent racism in the movement. However, I'm sure we would agree that being Christians transformed into the image of Christ most certainly can.

11

A Postmodern Christianity

Progressive "Christianity" is the point at which all these postmodern beliefs run headfirst into the Church, challenging biblical beliefs and, ultimately, creating a new religion. You will find all the usual suspects of deconstruction, the patriarchy, linguistic theft, oppression, and power structures within the conversation. You will also find an affinity for God's love that places this attribute above all else. Specifically, this is the belief system we discussed at the beginning of the book that separates sin and salvation through a focus on love.

For many, the reason they turn to this counterfeit gospel is simple. Layered on top of a foundation that lacked biblical and spiritual discipleship, Paul's second letter to Timothy expresses it well, *"For the time will come when men will not put up with sound doctrine. Instead, to suit their own desires, they will gather around them a great number of teachers to say what their itching ears want to hear. They will turn their ears away from the truth and turn aside to myths"* (2 Timothy 4:3–4).

Beyond appealing to people who want to stay safe in their sin, many stories of people who veer toward progressive "Christianity" include:

- Some level of Church hurt caused by other believers or those in Church leadership.
- Rejection of LGBTQ+ lifestyle, either personally or witnessing someone else rejected by the Church or their Christian family for that reason.
- Legalistic belief systems that have created an environment of fear and unforgiveness in the Church rather than grace.

The Church isn't perfect, and the hurt, whether real or perceived, led some to reject the Church as a whole and the Christian faith because of it. Others, rather than desert it altogether, found a new gospel that takes the sting out of the gospel of Christ, particularly the parts that offend or are difficult to defend. God's love becomes His most revered attribute because, according to this ideology, love does not offend and therefore has nothing to defend.

However, the gospel is offensive. Even Jesus said, *"I did not come to bring peace, but a sword. ... anyone who does not take his cross and follow me is not worthy of me"* (Matthew 10:34-39). He calls people to repent (turn) from their sins, count the costs, and obey Him. Jesus was not trying to make friends. He was saving humankind from eternal separation from Him due to sin.

The reason God called us to build Genuine Family Ministries is because of progressive "Christianity" and the anti-biblical ideas entering the Church and Christian homes. If we as parents are not raising our kids on a biblical foundation, then we will lose our children and the Church in the next generation to progressive postmodern ideology. We may still have church buildings, but they will not profess Jesus Christ and His death, burial, and Resurrection to cover our sins and reconcile us to a holy God.

With some believers being "*tossed back and forth by the waves, and blown here and there by every wind of teaching,*" as Paul describes in Ephesians 4:14, we must consider how our families will stand firm amid the assault.

To understand the framework of progressive "Christianity," Alisa Childers highlights five components in her first podcast. Below are her points (bolded), along with some of my observations.[38]

1. **For starters, with progressive "Christianity," there is a lowered view of the Bible.** The belief is that God did not divinely inspire the Bible but that the Jewish patriarchy wrote it.

   Therefore, the Bible is man's perspective of God, not who God really is, and is subject to error.

   This relates to a common belief in postmodernism that truth is unknowable and is subject to each individual's truth. This idea then gets applied to the writers of the Bible to invalidate their writings and understanding of God.

   This component alone is problematic because if there's no standard for truth (i.e., the Bible), then we decide what truth is to us individually. We base our beliefs about God on our feelings versus the facts, which leads to point two.

2. **Feelings become the ultimate authority.** It's common to hear people ask, "What does that verse mean to you?" rather than "What is God telling us in this verse?" It's that idea in postmodernism where the reader, rather than the author, defines the meaning. It's more about my interpretation than what God intended.

3. **Essential Christian doctrines are open for reinterpretation.** For example, is Jesus actually the Son of God, did He have to die on the Cross, did the Resurrection really happen, was His death on the Cross for our sins or because there was a power-hungry mob after Him? Doctrines get reinterpreted to fit a new narrative.

4. **Historic terms are redefined.** Childers gives the example that people in progressive Christian camps may use terms like inerrancy, infallibility, and inspiration of Scripture, but with new definitions. So, while we may be using the exact same words, we could be talking about two very different things — linguistic theft at its finest.

5. **The gospel shifts from sin and redemption to social justice.** In this sense, Jesus didn't come to atone for our sins but to bring down power structures to help the oppressed.

The oppressed today, specifically, are those who identify as LGBTQ+, women, and people of color. As such, the celebration and normalization of the LGBTQ+ lifestyle, the pro-choice movement, and racial reconciliation efforts are typically hallmarks of progressive Christian churches. To be clear, as the Church we should focus on loving people well, all without sacrificing biblical truth. However, that's not what happens in progressive "Christian" churches. Rather, the postmodern ideas of critical gender, queer, and race theories become the solution rather than the Word of God.

These first four points from the previous list are essentially the ingredients for deconstruction to occur because they break down history, core beliefs, and the meaning of words, and then put the interpretation in the hands of the observer. The fifth point is the new narrative that takes shape to reconstruct the gospel.

The primary progressive "Christian" ideas that have flowed from this framework include:

- Questioning the deity of Christ and the goodness of God.
- Unhitching the Old Testament from the New Testament. In other words, disregarding the Old Testament primarily because it highlights God's anger and His justice toward sin.
- With the unhitching of the Old Testament comes the unhitching of the atonement for sin as a core doctrine of the faith.
- Without the need to atone for (cover) sins, what we discover in Jesus is a good, kind, loving man who loved and ate with sinners and spoke truth to power. Love becomes His defining attribute, and social justice becomes His mission.
- Since His purpose is to love people unconditionally and set the oppressed free, His deity is unnecessary, just His example and activism on behalf of the oppressed.
- Jesus then becomes a moral man who did good things, and people embrace Him because of His good deeds, love, and justice work, not because He is Savior and Lord.

That sums up the progressive "Christian movement." There will inevitably be variations because so much depends on personal experience and interpretation. Some will focus more on love, others more on justice. However, anywhere you find the pride flag flying outside a church, you'll find these beliefs thriving, along with a reluctance to share the gospel of sin and salvation and, generally, a denial of it altogether.

One post I saw around Christmastime by a progressive "Christian" highlights this movement well. It said, "Why do we think Mary was meek and mild? She agreed to bear a child out of wedlock in defiance of her culture. She sang a song of liberation and freedom for the oppressed and unjustly treated. She made a rough journey to Bethlehem when heavily pregnant and another to Egypt with an infant. She was a revolutionary, a fitting mother for her rebel son."

To be clear, Jesus does not identify as a rebel, a revolutionary, an antiracist, feminist, nationalist, Marxist, or capitalist. He identifies as God.

Of all the false doctrines out there, progressive "Christianity" is one of the most dangerous for one simple reason: it disassociates sin from the gospel. It portrays a loving God who does not require justice to atone for sin because His unconditional love covers all. Played out to its logical conclusion, this means Jesus did not need to die on the Cross because the Cross was God's justice on display to cover the sins of all who believe. If God didn't require justice for sin in the world, then He didn't require Jesus to walk this earth. It denies the very sacrifice, forgiveness, and redemption of Jesus.

So, how do we stand firm in an environment where false ideologies enter the Church, and how do we equip our children to do the same? We can equip our kids to identify false doctrines/teachings, educate them on God's character, and teach them who Jesus is.

Identifying False Doctrines/Teachings

One of the easiest ways to teach our kids to identify a false doctrine is to recognize the character of God elevated above the rest. For example, when we focus on:

Wrath	We get hail, fire, and brimstone. We get an unforgiving, unrelenting Father and question our salvation every time we sin.
Love	We get progressive "Christianity." We get a Jesus who loves us unconditionally and supports whatever life decisions we make because He is here for us and loves us dearly and, ultimately, because He made us this way.
Justice	We get liberation theology. We get a Jesus who came to set the captives free and shut down all the power structures to ensure there's equality for all in the world. (This belief now merges with progressive "Christianity.")
Goodness and Grace	We get the prosperity gospel. We get a God who wants to bless us, and if we have enough faith, He will reward us with prosperity, riches, healing, and power.
Holiness and Order	We get a Pharisee mindset. We get a God with a list that He constantly checks to ensure we are as perfect as possible and where there is no room for error or grace.

The Character of God

Whenever we focus solely on one attribute of God, we will get a false gospel because God is not one-dimensional. He has many characteristics, specifically seven, that are necessary for us and our kids to know and understand for the gospel to make any sense.

God is:	
Ordered	God is the Creator and has designed the world to work in a certain way (Genesis 1). God determines what is good or righteous and what is evil or sin (Exodus 20).
Holy	God is perfect, pure, and without blemish, meaning there is no sin found in Him (Leviticus 19:2). God hates sin.
Just	God has a standard of what is good (right, moral, righteous) before Him (Deuteronomy 32:4). His justice is the administration of what is correct and righteous before Him based on how He has ordered the world. God's justice requires a consequence for sin (Genesis 3).
Love	God's love sent Jesus to the Cross to atone for the sins of all who believe. God's justice required the Cross, including His death, burial, and Resurrection (John 3:16).
Judge	God judges what is good and evil and has given Jesus authority to make a ruling for each individual (John 5:27).

Grace	God's grace covers those who believe in Jesus as Lord and Savior. That faith makes us holy before God and reconciles (reunites) us to Him (Ephesians 2:8).
Wrath	God's wrath is for all those who reject Him. The lack of faith in Jesus as Lord and Savior will create eternal separation from His love and goodness (Matthew 25:41).

If we remove any of these characteristics, which false gospels often do, we will get an inaccurate gospel. Some false gospels don't threaten our salvation, but they negatively impact how we live a Christian life. Consider the hell, fire, and brimstone approach. Believing you can lose your salvation, for example, doesn't make you lose your salvation, but it can make you live in fear, not realizing the complete peace of God. A false gospel like progressive "Christianity," on the other hand, can threaten your salvation because it denies the work of Christ to atone for sin, which is the foundation of our faith.

Who Is Jesus?

We also need to understand who Jesus is, because the current narrative strips Jesus of His deity. If Jesus is a good man whose example we should follow, but we don't need to obey Him, then He is not Lord and Savior, but a role model.

So, who is Jesus?

- **He is God.**

Jesus made the exclusive claim that He was one with God and that God was His Father. Jesus also calls Himself the "*Alpha and the Omega"* in Revelation 1:8, a phrase used to describe God. He forgave sins as only God could do. Paul says, *"For in Christ all the fullness of the Deity lives in bodily form"* (Colossians 2:9). The disciples professed He was God, as did the demons. The Pharisees mockingly crowned Him "King of the Jews" because they knew who He claimed to be. Most notably, God verified this claim after Jesus' baptism and transfiguration when God said, *"This is my Son, whom I love; with him I am well pleased"* (Matthew 3:17, 17:5).

- **His life on earth was for a specific purpose.**

Scripture outlines God's requirement for a blood sacrifice to atone for (cover) sin. The animal sacrifice had to be blemish-free (without defect), which is why Jesus' life on earth was without sin — so that He could be the perfect sacrifice and His shed blood could atone for our sins. As sin entered the world through one man, Adam, so one man, Jesus, the Son of God, covered that sin for all who believe (Romans 5:12–19).

- **He died, was buried, and resurrected to life.**

In Romans 1:4, Paul declares that Jesus is known to be the Son of God because of His Resurrection. He also tells us that our faith is useless if Christ didn't rise from the dead (1 Corinthians 15:17). Why? Because if Christ didn't rise from the dead, then death overcame Him, He did not triumph over sin and Satan, and He was not God.

When talking to our kids about the Bible, we need to reiterate that it is a history book, not a fiction book full of "characters" and "stories," but facts about people who lived and their history. The Bible is the history of Israel, a nation that exists today, and our Lord and Savior, and it describes how the Christian faith spread worldwide. We also need to reiterate that it's one book inspired by

God from start to finish. In it, God reveals what we need to know about creation, the Fall, salvation (redemption), and restoration.

As such, it is also the evidence of the Resurrection because it includes eyewitness accounts – in other words, the history of Jesus' Resurrection from people who were there. In Acts 2:32, Peter confirms, "*God has raised this Jesus to life, and we are all witnesses of the fact.*" Peter also reminds us that King David had prophesied "*the resurrection of the Christ, that he was not abandoned to the grave, nor did his body see decay*" (Acts 2:31). Not only were there eyewitnesses, but the miraculous event also fulfilled a prophecy given to David a thousand years prior to Jesus' life on earth.

The disciples' response was one of the most telling proofs of the Resurrection. Before seeing Jesus resurrected, they hid in the upper room, afraid of the authorities. After seeing Jesus resurrected, they proclaimed Him with no fear; most notably, all of the Apostles were willing to die for their testimony, and many did.

Teaching our kids to spot false doctrines, the character of God, and who Jesus is will equip them to stand for truth in a culture that encourages them to fight for lies. It takes intention and time to equip our kids. However, your family, your children's family, their children's family, and the Church are worth every second.

> *Let us not become weary in doing good, for at the proper time we will reap a harvest if we do not give up* (Galatians 6:9).

12

Raising Them to Stand

The best apologetic of all time is a life changed, one where there is evidence of the Holy Spirit's transforming work in our life and where people can see that what we preach, we actually believe. Not because our changed life saves, only Jesus does that, but because our changed life means our faith is genuine. We are not hypocrites, putting on a mask and pretending to be someone else or believing something that we don't.

The commoditized gospel that many of us grew up with did not encourage us to search after God, to learn His Word, to spend time in His presence, and to allow the Holy Spirit to change us. It didn't even tell us what faith really meant — it's not a temporary high and moment of peace, but an assuredness of what is real and true and found only in Jesus. Most of us don't get that level of faith in a moment and a prayer, but only after digging in and pursuing God.

Instead, we learn that the gospel is easy and requires nothing from us because grace covers all, and works are not all that important in the Kingdom. In other words, I can continue living exactly how I have, and God's okay with that.

Others grew up with a gospel that only preached works, checklists, and productivity. We came to believe that our heart change was unimportant as long as we were doing good for the Kingdom of God through our activity and strict adherence to rules. We may have never heard of God's grace and only heard of His holiness.

When we focus only on one part of God, we miss and see past all the Scriptures that push us to something more — the passages that tell us something more complete about God and His expectations of us as followers of Christ. For starters, there *are* expectations, and there's also grace. There should be evidence in our lives of change, not perfection, but of someone different because we are a new creation in Christ.

Jesus lets us know that how we live this life matters to the Kingdom of God and that He requires more than just a sedentary Sunday school life from us. He said to us,

- *"'Love the Lord your God with all your heart and with all your soul and with all your mind.' This is the first and greatest commandment"* (Matthew 22:37–38)
- *"Enter through the narrow gate. For wide is the gate and broad is the road that leads to destruction, and many enter through it. But small is the gate and narrow the road that leads to life, and only a few find it"* (Matthew 7:13–14).

- *"If anyone would come after me, he must deny himself and take up his cross and follow me"* (Matthew 16:24).
- *"But everyone who hears these words of mine and does not put them into practice is like a foolish man who built his house on sand. The rain came down, the streams rose, and the winds blew and beat against that house, and it fell with a great crash"* (Matthew 7:26–27)
- *"Not everyone who says to me, 'Lord, Lord,' will enter the kingdom of heaven, but only the one who does the will of my Father who is in heaven"* (Matthew 7:21).
- *"My sheep listen to my voice; I know them, and they follow me. I give them eternal life, and they shall never perish; no one can snatch them out of my hand"* (John 10:27–28).
- *"But the one who received the seed that fell on good soil is the man who hears the word and understands it. He produces a crop, yielding a hundred, sixty or thirty times what was sown"* (Matthew 13:23).
- *"Do not store up for yourselves treasures on earth, where moths and vermin destroy, and where thieves break in and steal. But store up for yourselves treasures in heaven, where moths and vermin do not destroy, and where thieves do not break in and steal. For where your treasure is, there your heart will be also"* (Matthew 6:19–21).

These verses matter because if we want to raise our kids to stand, we must first stand. We must be fortified for the fire and know where our hope comes from. We cannot expect our kids to go where we haven't gone or to believe a Christian life is the best life worth living if we don't believe it.

Our walk with Christ and our daily time with Him matters to the Kingdom of God, this next generation, and our legacy. It also matters to the preservation of the faith. If it sounds like a lot depends on us, that's because it does. We are shepherding a generation that needs to turn the trend of the declining Christian faith in the U.S. For the first time, more people have no religious affiliation in the country than those who claim Christianity.[39] For Christians to stand apart, stand out, stand up, and stand against the enemy, the power of Christ working in our lives must change us.

Research consistently shows that "The most powerful influence on the religious lives of American teenagers and young adults is the religious lives of their parents. Not their peers, not the media, not their youth group leaders," according to *Handing Down the Faith*.[40] It's YOU. It's ME. And our personal walk with Jesus has a significant impact on how our children perceive the faith.

Sometimes, I think about the importance of legacy to God — the prayers, spiritual life, and Kingdom work of one family and the impact it has on generations to come. Just consider how one man and one woman come together in marriage. They have two kids, those two kids each have two kids, those kids each have two kids, and those kids each have two kids. Within five generations alone, one man and one woman can easily have a family line of thirty people. That family, rooted in the Christian faith, can significantly impact the Kingdom. It reminds me why the family is so important and why the enemy hates it so much. There's a compounding effect of generational legacy to the Christian faith, and it's important to God.

So, how will we raise our kids to stand?

Raised to Stand Apart

> *I am the true vine, and my Father is the gardener. He cuts off every branch in me that bears no fruit, while every branch that does bear fruit he prunes so that it will be even more fruitful* (John 15:1–2)

Raising our kids to stand apart will mean that they understand that their relationship with Jesus Christ is the most essential thing, and they will pursue the Holy Spirit's sanctifying (purifying) work in their lives. They will make choices against the grain and be sensitive to the Holy Spirit's conviction. They will allow God to work in them even when it's hard, and recognize that their struggles will produce fruit.

The journey will not be easy, but rest assured that they will know there's more to life than grades, sports, drama, cell phones, social media, friends, and college acceptance. It's their relationship with Christ, and the work He wants to do through them is the priority. A love like this for Christ will only happen through our children's own decisions. They alone are responsible for their faith walk, but what we can do is model a life like this. We can tell our kids what the Lord is doing in our lives, how He's convicting us, the changes we are making and praying for in our lives. We can also recognize and point out the changes we see in them. We also pray for our kids to have this kind of love for God, one that decides to put God on the throne in their life and then consistently put Him back there when the pace of this world distracts or the troubles of this world drown them for a time.

Raised to Stand Up

> *Whoever acknowledges me before men, I will also acknowledge him before my Father in heaven. But whoever disowns me before men, I will disown him before my Father in heaven. Do not suppose that I have to come to bring peace to the earth. I did not come to bring peace, but a sword* (Matthew 10:32–34).

Equipped kids are bold — bottom line. The kids who stand up in their schools and share the love of Christ in their communities are not the ones just going to church on Sunday. They seek after Christ personally, find discipleship relationships, use their giftings, create accountability circles with their friends, and focus on their sanctification.

It's their knowledge of Scripture and their relationship with Jesus that creates a boldness to share Him with others. They know what they know, and they will not back down because they know it. There is a fire deep in their souls and a conviction that does not waver. For kids to stand up, we must equip them. No one has ever effectively stood without knowing what they were standing for.

Everything we've covered so far will equip our kids to stand up. Knowledge is an integral part of God's transformational work in our lives. Our minds must be set on God above and we should not to be conformed *"any longer to the pattern of this world, but be transformed by the renewing of your mind"* (Romans 12:2). That's what equipping our kids with theology, worldview, apologetics, and critical thinking skills will do. They will learn to discern false teachings, correct wrong beliefs, and bring people along on the faith journey.

Even though they may desperately desire to fit in, they will also recognize that what Jesus said is true, *"If the world hates you, keep in mind that it hated me first ... As it is, you do not belong to the world, but I have chosen you out of the world"* (John 15:18–19).

To equip our kids, we have to be intentional. It doesn't mean we have to have an hour dedicated each day to discipleship. However, it does mean we need to ensure our kids receive education on Scripture and worldview and that we intentionally have conversations with them about God's work in our lives and what the Bible says. Committing ourselves to being faithful in our time with God and learning His Word will go a long way to fill us up so we can pour into our kids.

Raised to Stand Out

> *You are the light of the world. A city on a hill cannot be hidden. Neither do people light a lamp and put it under a bowl. Instead they put it on its stand, and it gives light to everyone in the house. In the same way, let your light shine before men, that they may see your good deeds and praise your Father in heaven* (Matthew 5:14–16).

There's no more powerful way for our kids to share their faith with the next generation than to have conversations in truth and love. The days when we spew vitriol on our social media posts or in the comments section are long gone and were never effective. The world is desperate for our light. Even if it takes them time to see it, if our kids are consistently shining bright, their friends will know where to turn when the darkness gets too bleak and the Holy Spirit calls.

Teaching our kids how to live by the Spirit and to keep in step with the Spirit will help them discern how God wants them to engage in conversations and relationships with unbelievers or those who are actively living in sin. Reminding our kids to pray when they have a friend who is hurting, confused, or even disrespectful to the gospel will remind them that God is in control and that compassion and love should be our first response. It is essential to encourage them to speak the truth when the Holy Spirit calls and not feel ashamed. That is because being all about love but never speaking the truth of sin and salvation never saved a soul. Relationships are critical, and our kids need to understand that they do not have to say everything in their first conversation, but that as the relationship grows and they follow the Holy Spirit, God will guide them in all truth and love.

Raised to Stand Against

> *"Light has come into the world, but men loved darkness instead of light because their deeds were evil. Everyone who does evil hates the light, and will not come into the light for fear that his deeds will be exposed"* (John 3:19–21).

There's absolutely no doubt that Satan and his evil ways are on full display in our world today. Our kids need to know this, too. That there's a spiritual realm, and it's not only God and His angels that live in it. Satan is alive and well, too, and has one mandate: to kill, steal, and destroy. When evil abounds, the enemy is present, and it rejects the light. When our kids actively stand for God, they will have a target on them.

The best help we can provide our kids in these situations is to understand the signs of spiritual warfare so we can discern what's happening and pray. The devil's only language is lies, and that's precisely what Jesus told us of him. As such, spiritual attacks usually come on quickly and have an oppressive feeling about them, creating despair, hopelessness, an overall down and depressive feeling, irrational thoughts, or harsh self-criticism. His attacks never include joy, peace, or the Lord's love, which is how to spot them. Once you notice it, pray for your child's protection and have them pray. Just as quickly as spiritual attacks come on, they can leave, which is one way to differentiate them from mental health situations like anxiety or depression.

Scripture also tells us how to protect ourselves from the enemy's schemes. *"Finally, be strong in the Lord and in his mighty power. Put on the full armor of God so that you can take your stand against the devil's schemes. For our struggle is not against flesh and blood, but against the rulers, against the authorities, against the powers of this dark world and against the spiritual forces of evil in the heavenly realms. Therefore put on the full armor of God, so that when the day of evil comes, you may be able to stand your ground ..."* (Ephesians 6:10–13). Scripture says that God's Word, truth, and faith are all ways we can take our stand against the enemy's schemes.

Faith-Filled Family

It may or may not surprise some to learn how unstructured we are as a family. Sure, we have our family rhythms, but not a lot runs like clockwork in our family, especially mealtimes. I used to feel like such a failure that we weren't the family who ate around the dinner table. The reality is that all of our family lives are very different, including our strengths, giftings, and dynamics. When God brought two people together as husband and wife, a new family and traditions formed.

Not long ago, someone asked me to be part of a speaker series to share how we raised Christian kids in our home. The organizer invited several families to speak who all had children living out their Christian faith in their schools, neighborhoods, and churches.

One day during our planning session for it, as I listened to the other moms talk about the parenting books they read and methodologies they had tried, I began to feel unworthy of being part of this conversation because I hadn't read any of those books or tried any of those methods. Even now, I remember vividly that feeling of inadequacy.

It took me a little bit of time to remember that God knew the parent I would be. He can amplify our wins and cover our missteps. He is sovereign over all, and He knows the plans He has for us.

If you ever feel inadequate, remember that God knew the parent you would be, too. He also knew the parent your child needed, and there's no better person than you. For example, my boys will get much more conversation about culture and worldview than most. For other kids, they are going to get a lot more nature walks and fishing lessons than their peers. Some children will get parents who love to laugh, get messy and crafty, and don't mind the cleanup. Each style allows us to reflect on God and teach His ways and Word.

Regardless of our styles, we can all create an environment in our homes where our kids hear the Word, learn the Word, and live the Word. You can schedule it like clockwork if that's your style, or you can be more in the moment if you're a bit like me; either way, the key is intentionality.

Some of the most important guiding principles in our home have been:	
Personal Relationship	Model a changed life through our own relationship with Jesus.
Be Present	Be available, accessible, and present in our kids' lives and create an environment that invites open conversation.
Point to God	Take opportunities to point to God through prayer, nature, Scripture, and life situations.
Priorities	Ensure our schedule, first and foremost, represents our faith priorities, including church activities.
Pray	Pray for their protection, salvation, sanctification, and friendships.

These five principles have kept our family grounded in Christ. Deciding your guiding family principles can keep you on track when the days get busy and overwhelming. It won't always be perfect, but it will point us in the right direction to correct course when needed.

Conclusion

Raising Christian kids in a postmodern world is daunting sometimes. We worry about the ideas our kids get exposed to, the friends who have come into their lives, and if they will make the good decisions that we hope they will. There's a lot to consider and stress over, mainly because of the changes in our culture. The reality is, though, that there is no Jr. Holy Spirit. The same Holy Spirit we receive when we are saved is the same one our kids receive. The Holy Spirit will guide them in truth, convict them of sin, and comfort them when hurt. The God of all creation is still on the throne, and Jesus is still the Savior of the world. Yes, the world is increasingly dark, but the light shines all the brighter in the darkness.

What if raising Christian kids in this culture was the greatest honor that God could have ever given us? To steward our kids and this next generation into the next great move of God. Raising pillars of faith who will stand when the ground is shaky, the pressure is heavy, and the world is taking a proverbial nosedive — the faithful who will rise, who will stand, who will profess our Lord Jesus, who will love their neighbor, and will stand firmly on God's Word, and who will then raise their kids to do the same. Maybe we will be the generation of parents who turned it all around — who saw where things were heading, made the sacrifice, and answered the call to raise a different kind of Christian, ones who wouldn't back down and who would never give up until they accomplished all that God had called them to. Ones who we raised to stand.

Glossary

Please note that there are general definitions, postmodern definitions that reflect a more secular perspective, and feminist definitions that reflect meaning from that perspective.

Allies (postmodern definition): People who align themselves with people in the oppressed categories and champion social justice causes.

Apologetics: The skill of learning to defend the faith.

Apologia: Greek word that translates to a defense of the gospel in the current culture (aka society).

Atonement: The forgiveness, or covering, of our sins through Jesus' blood sacrifice.

Binary: A belief in two categories (specifically male and female).

Bodily autonomy (feminist definition): The concept that people have the right to make decisions over their own lives and bodies and should be able to do so (e.g., abortion rights).

Cisgender (postmodern definition): Someone whose gender identity matches their biological sex (e.g., a person who identifies as a man and is biologically a man).

Coming-out parties (postmodern definition): An event celebrating a person's LGBTQ+ identity.

Culture: Comes from the word "cultivate," which refers to what we grow, build, and enhance in our world.

Deadnaming (postmodern definition): Using someone's birth name and not their new preferred name.

Deconstruction (postmodern definition): Destroying or tearing down social constructs, including ideas and institutions, such as the justice system.

Disciple: In Hebrew means "learners" or "scholars."

Diversity, Equity, and Inclusion (DEI) (postmodern definition): Programs, typically introduced in businesses, government, and other organizations, meant to create equity and elevate oppressed voices as equal, or in most cases, more important than those who fall into oppressor categories.

Equity (postmodern definition): Equal outcomes, not equal opportunities, for minority groups.

Furries (postmodern definition): People interested in anthropomorphized animals and dressing up like them.

Gender dysphoria (postmodern definition): A feeling of distress that results when someone believes their gender identity doesn't match his or her biological sex.

Gender expression (postmodern definition): Representing one's gender identity through clothing, hairstyle, voice, body shape, etc.

Gender fluid (postmodern definition): A person who does not confine themselves to one gender or another.

Gender identity (postmodern definition): One's internal sense of being male, female, neither of these, both, or another gender(s).

Intersectionality (postmodern definition): The practice of looking at the intersection of race, gender, class (socioeconomic status), and (dis)ability to understand the compounding effects of being part of multiple minority or oppressed groups.

Justification: Made righteous (holy, without sin) before the Lord.

LGBTQQIA (postmodern definition): An extension to LGBTQ+ that includes lesbian, gay, bi (bisexual), trans, queer, questioning, intersex, asexual/agender.

Lived experience (postmodern definition): The personal experience of someone in an oppressed category.

Misgendering (postmodern definition): Not using someone's preferred pronouns.

Misogyny (feminist definition): Hatred, contempt, or prejudice against women.

Nonbinary (postmodern definition): Someone who does not conform to the binary of male or female.

Oppressed (postmodern definition): The people in society who do not have power and have suffered accordingly.

Oppressors (postmodern definition): People who have power in society, typically referring to the patriarchy.

Original sin: The belief that we all have inherited a sinful nature since birth, based on the first sin of Adam and Eve.

Pan (pansexual) (postmodern definition): Someone who is attracted to an individual regardless of gender, also considered gender-blind.

Patriarchy (postmodern definition): Old, rich white men who institute or enable power structures in society.

Queer (postmodern definition): Someone who does not conform to traditional beliefs about gender and sexual identity.

Reconciliation: Reuniting with God as a result of atonement and faith.

Reproductive rights (feminist definition): Ensuring legal rights for abortion and access to birth control.

Salvation: The saving of humans from sin (and the eternal consequences of sin) through faith in Jesus Christ as Lord and Savior.

Sanctification: The process of transforming into the image of Christ by the work of the Holy Spirit in our lives to purify us.

Science worldview (aka Naturalism): Based solely on logical thought and reason, excluding any possibility of a spiritual world or supernatural being.

Sex assigned at birth (postmodern definition): The assignment of people as male, female, or intersex based on a combination of anatomy, hormones, and chromosomes; biological sex.

Sexism (feminist definition): Discrimination against women based on sex (gender).

Sin: Disobedience to God's Word/commands.

Social constructs (postmodern definition): The idea that the patriarchy constructed society to work in a specific way, resulting in the creation of institutions, like marriage, and conventions, such as the binary of male and female.

Social justice warriors (postmodern definition): People who activate around the social justice causes of race, gender, and sexuality.

Social justice worldview (aka Postmodernism): Belief that the world consists of those in power, the oppressors, and those who do not have power, the oppressed. The only way to overturn those power structures is to deconstruct institutions in society.

Spiritual worldview (aka Transcendentalism): Focuses on emotions, feelings, and the inner self; supernatural is more real than the natural.

Submitted worldview (aka Theism): Hinges on the belief that there is a God who is personal and accessible, created the world, and fashioned humankind as finite beings who had a beginning and did not evolve.

TERF (postmodern definition): Derogatory term that stands for Trans Exclusionary Radical Feminists; feminists who support abortion and LGBTQ+ rights but oppose having trans women (biological men) take rights and experiences away from biological women.

Theology: The study of God through the Bible that helps us grasp the core beliefs of the Christian faith and the major themes we find in Scripture.

Toxic masculinity (feminist definition): Traditional male roles considered harmful, such as being dominant and aggressive.

Trans (postmodern definition): A person whose gender identity does not match their biological sex (e.g., a person who identifies as a man but is biologically a woman; a trans man).

Truth (postmodern definition): A person's experience determines their truth, including upbringing, family dynamics, religion, socioeconomic status, ethnicity, sexual and gender identity, and more.

Worldview: The lens through which we see the world and how we perceive it.

Endnotes

1. Trueman, Carl R. *Strange New World.* Wheaton: Crossway, 2022.
2. Ibid.
3. Childers, Alisa. *Another Gospel.* Carol Stream: Tyndale Elevate, 2020.
4. Morrow, Jonathan. *5 Surprising Facts About the Worldview of Gen Z.* Impact 360 Institute, 2018. https://www.impact360institute.org/podcasts/5-surprising-facts-worldview-gen-z/#:~:text=When%20Barna%20began%20studying%20the,Z%20have%20a%20biblical%20worldview.
5. Phillips, Gary W., Brown, William E., Stonestreet, John. *Making Sense of Your World.* Salem: Sheffield Publishing Company, 2008.
6. Colson, Charles, and Pearcey, Nancy. *How Now Shall We Live?* Carol Stream: Tyndale House Publishers, 1999.
7. Phillips, Gary W., Brown, William E., Stonestreet, John. *Making Sense of Your World.* Salem: Sheffield Publishing Company, 2008.
8. Colson, Charles, and Pearcey, Nancy. *How Now Shall We Live?* Carol Stream: Tyndale House Publishers, 1999.
9. Piper, John. "What does it mean to be made in God's Image?" Ask Pastor John, Episode 153. Apple Podcasts, August 19, 2013. https://www.desiringgod.org/interviews/what-does-it-mean-to-be-made-in-gods-image
10. Colson, Charles, and Pearcey, Nancy. *How Now Shall We Live?* Carol Stream: Tyndale House Publishers, 1999.
11. IMAGE OF GOD: Piper, John. "What does it mean to be made in God's Image?" Ask Pastor John, Episode 153. Apple Podcasts, August 19, 2013. https://www.desiringgod.org/interviews/what-does-it-mean-to-be-made-in-gods-image
12. Shenvi, Neil. "Social Justice, Critical Theory, and Christianity: Are They Compatible?" Webinar presented at Southeastern Baptist Theological Seminary, Wake Forest, March 3, 2020. https://cfc.sebts.edu/faith-and-culture/neil-shenvi-are-social-justice-critical-theory-and-christianity-compatible/
13. Ferrer, Hillary Morgan. *Mama Bear Apologetics* Eugene: Harvest House Publishers, 2019.
14. Meyer, Stephen C. "Philosopher of Science Stephen C Meyer Explores the Exciting Theory of Intelligent Design." YouTube, February 27, 2019. https://www.youtube.com/watch?v=tu93Mw4mtec
15. Colson, Charles, and Pearcey, Nancy. *How Now Shall We Live?* Carol Stream: Tyndale House Publishers, 1999.
16. Pruitt, Sarah. "What are the Four Waves of Feminism?" History.com, October 4, 2023. https://www.history.com/news/feminism-four-waves
17. Lui, Nakkiah. "All About Connections: Nakkiah Lui 'Fourth Wave of Feminism.'" YouTube.com, March 5, 2020. https://www.youtube.com/watch?v=s1Nhocl1eKI
18. Temby, Joy and White, Summer. "Feminism is Poison: Volume 1 Remix." Sheologians. Apple Podcasts, January 14, 2019. https://www.sheologians.com/feminism-poison-volume-1-remix/

19. Davis, Daniel. "How 50 Years of No-Fault Divorce Gave Us a Throwaway Culture." Dailysignal.com, September 3, 2019. https://www.dailysignal.com/2019/09/03/how-50-years-of-no-fault-divorce-gave-us-a-throwaway-culture/
20. Steinem, Gloria. "Redefining Feminism." Online Class presented by MasterClass, Masterclass.com, November 16, 2021.
21. Ibid.
22. McDowell, Sean. *Chasing Love*. Nashville: B&H Publishing Group, 2020.
23. Planned Parenthood. "How Do You Know If Someone Wants to Have Sex with You?" YouTube, September 21, 2015. https://youtu.be/qNN3nAevQKY
24. Stuckey, Allie Beth. "Biblical Marriage." Relatable Podcast, Episode 126. YouTube, June 17, 2019. https://www.youtube.com/watch?v=8FWxcLL0-UE
25. Ferrer, Hillary Morgan and Davison, Amy. *Mama Bear Apologetics Guide to Sexuality*. Eugene: Harvest House Publishers, 2021.
26. Pearcey, Nancy. *Love Thy Body*. Grand Rapids: Baker Books, 2018.
27. Butler, Judith. *Gender Trouble*. Abingdon: Routledge, 1990.
28. Shrier, Abigail. *Irreversible Damage*. Washington: Regnery Publishing, 2020.
29. Trans Student Educational Resources, 2015. "The Gender Unicorn." http://www.transstudent.org/gender.
30. Grant, Ian M. "Battle of the Brain: Men vs Women." Northwestern Medicine, nm.org. https://www.nm.org/healthbeat/healthy-tips/battle-of-the-brain-men-vs-women-infographic
31. Amen, Daniel. "7 Differences Between Male and Female Brains." Amenclinics.com, September 22, 2021. https://www.amenclinics.com/blog/7-differences-between-male-and-female-brains/
32. Axis. "Furries Explained: What is a Furry?" YouTube, September 7, 2023. https://www.youtube.com/watch?v=cvpuYWoHIGQ
33. Kendi, Ibram X. *How to Be an Antiracist*. New York City: One World, 2019.
34. Research by The Harvard Poll and HarrisX. Harvard CAPS-Harris Poll, December 13-14, 2023. https://harvardharrispoll.com/wp-content/uploads/2023/12/HHP_Dec23_KeyResults.pdf
35. Legal Defense Fund. A Revealing Experiment: Brown v Board and the Doll Test. Naacpldf.com. https://www.naacpldf.org/brown-vs-board/significance-doll-test
36. Guinness, OS. "Colson Center: OS Guinness." Webinar presented on Zoom, April, 5, 2021.
37. Kendi, Ibram X. *How to Be an Antiracist*. New York City: One World, 2019.
38. Childers, Alisa. "What is Progressive Christianity?" The Alisa Childers Podcast, Episode 1. Apple Podcasts, June 8, 2017.
39. Smith, Gregory A, et al. Religious 'Nones' in America: Who They Are and What They Believe. Pew Research Center, 2024. https://www.pewresearch.org/religion/2024/01/24/religious-nones-in-america-who-they-are-and-what-they-believe/
40. Smith, Christian and Adamczyk, Amy. *Handing Down the Faith*. New York: Oxford University Press, 2021.

Index